The Growth of Civilization in East Asia

Early civilization in the Far East is basically the story of the growth and development of ancient China, for it was from the basin of the Yellow River in North China that art, science and inventions spread to other parts of Asia. Peter Lum tells the history of Ch'in Shih Huang Ti, first Emperor of China, who built the Great Wall and made China into a single nation: of Confucius, whose philosophy was the strongest single influence on Chinese life for two thousand years: of Tang T'ai Tsung, perhaps China's greatest ruler; and of the great Mongol emperors including Genghis Khan, whose empire stretched from the Danube to the Pacific.

Here, too, is the history of early Japan, where Chinese culture had an early and lasting influence. We read of the Heian period, a time devoted to art and letters, to all things beautiful: of the rise of feudalism and the Samurai warriors; and the beginnings of the Tea Ceremony and the art of landscape gardening.

And in Korea, too, Chinese civilization spread from earliest times and shaped the culture of the country that formed a bridge between China and Japan for centuries.

Peter Lum has written an informative, concise account of Far Eastern civilization from Neolithic times to the fall of the Mongol Empire.

Tomb figure of a lady (T'ang Dynasty: 618–906 A.D.)—
Courtesy, the Trustees of the British Museum, London

The Growth of Civilization in East Asia

CHINA, JAPAN, AND KOREA
BEFORE THE 14TH CENTURY

by PETER LUM

S. G. PHILLIPS *New York*

Library of Congress Catalog Card Number 73-77311

SBN 87599-144-0

Designed by Bernard Schleifer

Manufactured in the United States of America

THIS BOOK IS gratefully dedicated to those who, with the utmost patience and long suffering, have given their time to read and to comment upon the manuscript, and whose wise advice has added enormously to the pleasure of writing it.

Acknowledgments

THE SENTENCE beginning on page 56 with "Confucius was . . .", the passage beginning on page 91 with "The Legalist . . .", and the paragraph beginning on page 146 with "In retrospect . . ." are quoted from John K. Fairbank and Edwin O. Reischauer, *East Asia: The Great Tradition,* vol. 1 of *A History of East Asian Civilization* (Boston: Houghton Mifflin Company, 1958).

The poem on page 83, entitled "Li Fu-jen," is quoted from Arthur Waley (translator), *One Hundred and Seventy Chinese Poems* (London: Constable & Co., 1918), with the permission of the present holder of the copyright, Random House, Inc./Alfred A. Knopf, Inc.

The poem on page 131, written by Tu Fu and translated under the title "Quatrain" by Hsieh Wen Tung, is quoted from Robert Payne (editor), *The White Pony: An Anthology of Chinese Poetry* (New York: The John Day Co., 1947).

The paragraph beginning on page 136 with "In sorrow . . .", a translation by Soame Jenyns, under the title "A Spring Prospect," of a poem by Tu Fu, is quoted from *Poems of the T'ang Dynasty* (London: John Murray, 1940).

Contents

Contents

List of Illustrations

List of Illustrations

List of Maps

The Growth of Civilization in East Asia

I

The Beginnings

THE STORY OF early Oriental civilization is basically the story of ancient China. It was from the river valleys of north China that ideas, inventions, art, and science—in fact everything that we mean by culture and civilization—spread to other parts of east Asia. Korea, Japan, and the Indochinese peninsula all adopted and adapted Chinese culture in their own ways.

This is not to suggest that the influence was entirely one-sided. There were, of course, other strands in the fabric of Oriental civilization. Rice, for instance, was introduced to China from the south; the technique of casting bronze may have come from the west. The jungle tribes of the Indochinese peninsula, the boatbuilders of the South Pacific islands, the nomads of northeast Asia—all made their contribution. But the dominant element from the beginning was undoubtedly Chinese.

Geographically, however, in spite of its great influence on neighboring lands, China is a natural unit somewhat isolated from the rest of the world. The Pacific Ocean on the east, the great mountain ranges of Tibet on the west, the rivers, mountains, and jungle of the south and southwest are formidable barriers. The northern boundary is more flexible, but there too the division between the northern steppes and the agricultural land of China was always clear even before the building of the Great Wall underlined it. The only way of reaching the Middle East and Europe overland lies across deserts and mountain ranges which are among the most terrifying on earth. It has always been a hazardous, often an impossible journey.

The land mass of China slopes from west to east, from the mountains to the coastal plain. Two great rivers, the Huang Ho, or Yellow River, and the Yangtze, as well as many lesser streams, flow down this slope, so that communication has always been easier from east to west, and vice versa, along the river valleys, than from north to south.

The first Chinese we know much about is Peking Man, *Sinanthropus pekinensis,* whose bones were discovered in 1927 not far from Peking and who is thought to have lived about 400,000 years ago. He had already discovered the use of fire, and he had certain Mongoloid features not found in other races of the world. It is tempting to think that the modern Chinese are descended directly from this remote ancestor, but there are too many gaps. It is only from Late Neolithic times, shortly before 2000 B.C., and thus appreciably later than the earliest Egyptian or Mesopotamian cultures, that a distinctive Chinese culture can be traced.

This developed along the basin of the Yellow River, near its junction with the river Wei. The Chinese were later to expand in various stages from this early heartland. By 1600 B.C. they had spread across the eastern plain and reached the sea. By about 1300 B.C. they were on the Yangtze, and by 1100 B.C. they had pushed south of that great river. Finally, in the third and sec-

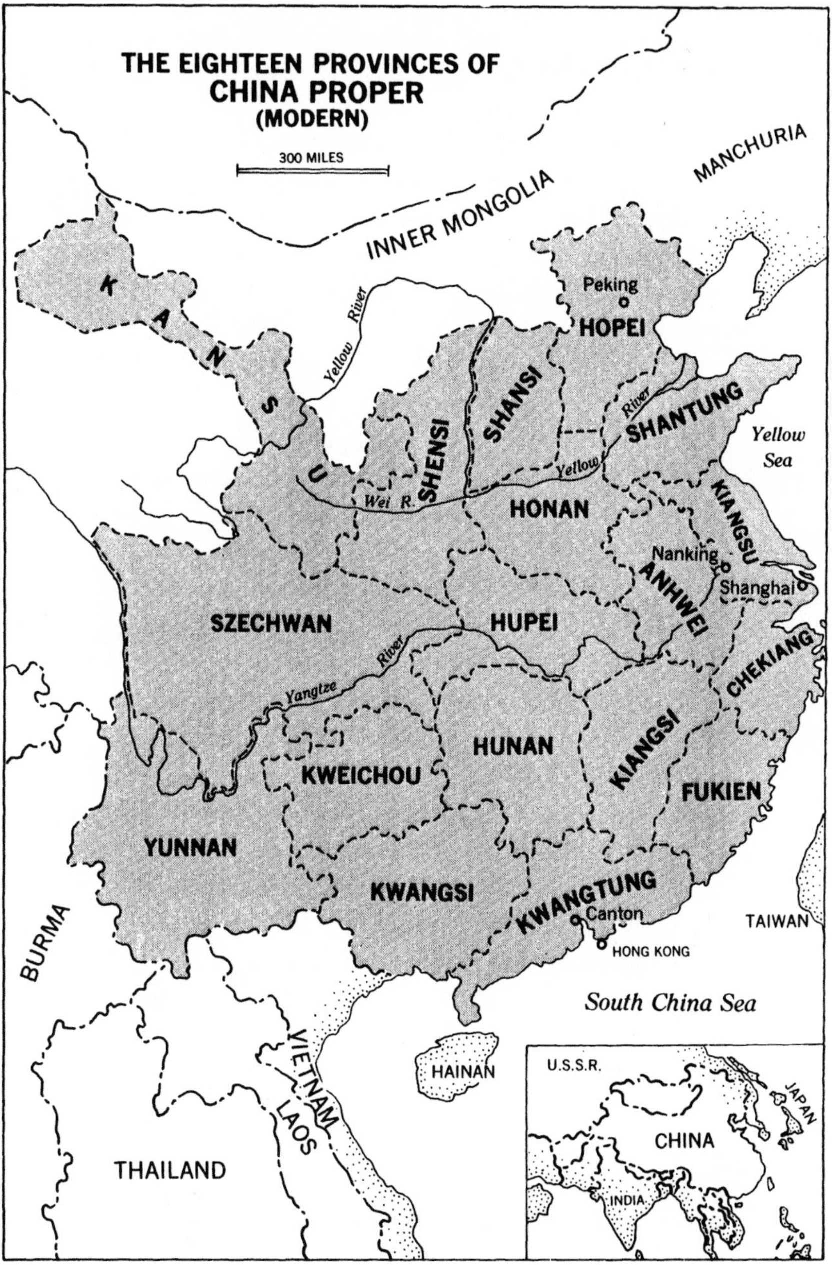
THE EIGHTEEN PROVINCES OF
CHINA PROPER
(MODERN)
300 MILES
INNER MONGOLIA
MANCHURIA
KANSU
Yellow River
Peking
HOPEI
SHANSI
SHENSI
SHANTUNG
River
Yellow
Yellow Sea
Wei R.
HONAN
KIANGSU
Nanking
ANHWEI
Shanghai
SZECHWAN
HUPEI
River
Yangtze
CHEKIANG
HUNAN
KIANGSI
KWEICHOU
FUKIEN
YUNNAN
KWANGSI
KWANGTUNG
Canton
TAIWAN
HONG KONG
BURMA
South China Sea
HAINAN
VIETNAM
LAOS
THAILAND
U.S.S.R.
JAPAN
CHINA
INDIA

ond centuries B.C., China expanded to something like its modern boundaries.

The Yellow River basin was in many ways an ideal situation. No great forests had to be cut down there before crops could be planted. The loose kind of soil called loess, the true "yellow earth" of China, which covered most of the western reaches, was easy to work, and it remained fertile, being constantly renewed by fresh, wind-borne deposits. Rainfall was scanty, but the great river provided water for the land and the crops—that is, if only it could be controlled.

The Yellow River, or Huang Ho, is an extraordinary river. It rises in mountains near the Tibetan border, so distant that legends say it flows from the Milky Way, and tell of fishermen who sailed too far west and found themselves in Heaven. After running in a great loop to the north, east, and south, it is joined by the Wei River, at which point it swings sharply east again, forming an "elbow" which is one of the most conspicuous features on the map of China. As it flows on across the broad plains of modern Shantung Province, largely built up over the centuries by silt from the river, it silts up its own bed until in some places it is as much as forty feet above the land, and must be held back by dikes. Throughout history millions of Chinese have lost their homes, their livelihood, and even their lives when the great river has burst its dikes and flooded the plain, earning the name "China's Sorrow." At times it may also alter its course by hundreds of miles, emptying into the sea now north, now south of the Shantung Peninsula. There was a major change of course as recently as 1851, and there have been two further shifts since then.

The first Yellow River culture, although it had its distinctive features, was similar to other Late Neolithic cultures. By 2000 B.C. its people had domesticated animals, first the pig and the dog, both of which they used for food, and later horses, sheep, and cattle. They were farmers, not nomads, and they lived in shallow, circular pit dwellings scraped out of the earth. Their weapons included bows and arrows, stone knives and axes, and in particular a curved, "semi-lunar" stone knife of a style found only in east Asia. They wove baskets and cloth, and they already had silk.

Millet was the chief crop, as it has always been in north China. The cultivation of wheat came slightly later, as did that of rice, although the latter is better suited to the climate of south China. Being an agricultural society, the religion of these early people probably included gods of the soil and grain-gods, as well as vague animistic beliefs attributing life to natural phenomena and to inanimate objects.

Metal was unknown, but the Neolithic Chinese already used jade for ornaments and for certain symbolic objects. The Chinese love, almost worship, of jade is constant throughout their history. But its use so early is remarkable. It is a very hard stone (the Chinese say that the best jade is crystallized moonlight) and difficult to cut with any tool. Moreover, the principal sources of jade are outside China proper, and it can never have been plentiful.

Like other Neolithic peoples, these early Chinese produced excellent pottery. There were three types, an early gray pottery and two quite different later varieties. One of these, the Painted Pottery, is characterized

Painted Pottery style

by bold designs, usually black on red, and is found mainly in the northwest. The other, a shiny Black Pottery, is found farther east and may be somewhat later in date.

Among the earliest pottery shapes is one exclusively Chinese: the *li*. This is a tripod, with hollow legs. One theory is that it originated in three pots with pointed bottoms being placed to lean together over a fire, whereupon someone had the bright idea of making all

Li pottery shape

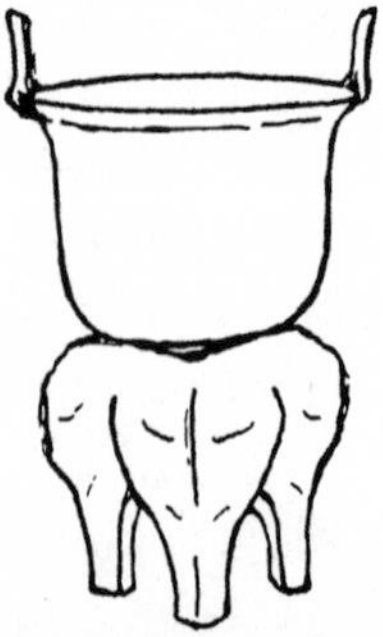

Hsien pottery shape

three together. Related to this, and equally ancient, is a sort of double boiler (called *hsien*): the lower half, a tripod, is filled with water, while the upper half has a perforated bottom for the steam to rise through.

There is no evidence of writing at this time, but it is reasonable to assume that the language of north China in Neolithic times was already Chinese. When writing does first appear, it is an archaic but clearly recognizable version of the script we know now.

Where no written records remain, myth and legend can tell us a great deal. According to Chinese mythology, the world began when P'an Ku, the first created being, separated Earth from Heaven. After P'an Ku died, his breath became the wind, his blood formed rivers, his eyes became the sun and moon, and all the earth's vegetation grew from his hair. This story was probably never taken very seriously, but Chinese historians do attribute the beginning of civilization to a series of rulers of the third millennium B.C., who may or may not also be mythological. Their reigns were impossibly long, their deeds were heroic, their births usually supernatural, but that does not necessarily prove that they did not exist.

Fu Hsi, with the aid of his sister Nu Kua, is said to have taught men to hunt, fish, and tame animals for domestic use, to wear clothing, and to cook their food. He invented writing, a calendar, and music, noting that the last had a soothing effect upon mankind.

Fu Hsi's successor, Shen Nung, taught men to plow, and even in this century the Emperors of China used to plow one furrow of soil each New Year's Day in memory of Shen Nung. He introduced the study of medicine, the extraction of salt from sea water, and the custom of holding markets where men could exchange their produce with one another.

Shen Nung was followed by Huang Ti, or the Yellow Emperor. (Yellow is the color of earth, the element

Detail from a stone engraving (Han Dynasty: 206 B.C.–220 A.D.) showing Fu Hsi, first of the mythical Chinese rulers, and his sister Nu Kua. Fu Hsi, on the right, holds a square, and Nu Kua holds a compass, symbolizing their bringing of order to the world under whose influence he was believed to rule.) He showed men how to build chariots and boats, and there is a remarkable story that once after the Emperor's army had lost its way in thick fog he "constructed a chariot upon which was mounted a prominent figure with arm outstretched, and which always pointed south whatever might be the direction taken by the chariot. By these south-pointing chariots . . . Huang Ti led his soldiers to victory."

From this it can be argued that the Chinese already had some form of compass over 4,000 years ago. South-pointing chariots are also said to have been in use during the tenth century B.C. Western engineers who have studied the description of these chariots believe that they had nothing to do with a magnetic compass, but that the Chinese might have invented a mechanism somewhat like the differential gear of modern cars, enabling the figure to point in the same direction regardless of how the chariot turned.

Huang Ti's wife meanwhile taught Chinese women how to raise silkworms, and how to spin the silk from their cocoons. And whatever the case for the compass, there is no doubt that the manufacture and use of silk was a very early Chinese invention, unknown elsewhere until silkworms were smuggled out to the West in the sixth century A.D.

Huang Ti was succeeded by a number of lesser rulers, of whom little is recorded. Then came the golden age of the Model Emperors, Yao, Shun, and Yü, when perfect harmony is said to have existed between Heaven and Earth. All men were brothers then. Each ruler handed on the throne to the best-qualified man alive. Thus Yao chose Shun as his successor when he learned that, although Shun's father was blind, stubborn, and wicked, his stepmother quarrelsome, and his half-brother arrogant, Shun himself was so virtuous that he lived in harmony with them all. To make quite sure of his quality, Yao gave his own two daughters to Shun in marriage, and this paragon lived happily with them both.

Yet there were problems even in that golden age: in particular, flood control.

"Destructive are the waters in their flood," lamented the Emperor Yao. "They embrace the mountains and overtop the hills . . . so that the inferior people groan and murmur. Is there a man to whom I can assign the correction of this calamity?"

His advisers recommended one Kun, and the Emperor summoned Kun, saying: "Go, and be reverent!"

Kun worked for nine years to control the flood of the Yellow River—probably by building dams—and failed. Then the Emperor Shun handed on the task to Kun's son Yü. And Yü devoted himself so singlemindedly to his work that it is said he would not stop to rest for thirteen years, even when he passed his own house and heard his wife's voice within.

Yü's method was to dig channels and deepen the existing canals, rather than trying to dam the flood. He was so successful that on Shun's death he was chosen Emperor. However, he handed on the throne to his own son, thus establishing both the hereditary principle and the first dynasty in Chinese records, the Hsia. (Since the Model Emperors must be perfect, later writers claimed that Yü gave the throne to his son only because the son was the person best qualified to rule, but one may have doubts about that.)

The efforts of Yü, or of whoever first did tame the Yellow River, profoundly influenced the pattern of Chinese life. For the work involved in flood control was not only enormous; it required organization. Dikes had to be built and canals dredged. Special skills had to be developed: astronomy for foretelling the coming of the floods, geometry for measuring the flow. Building materials had to be transported, which meant building roads.

Such large-scale operations had to be centrally controlled. This led to one man's having supreme power: to call out gangs of workers when needed; to requisition materials; to decide what work should be done, where, and when. It led, in fact, to dictatorship. The ruler must have absolute power over the people for their own sake.

An interesting theory is that it was this need for organized labor which enabled the rulers of such a so-called "hydraulic" society to go on and build the great monuments of the ancient world. The pyramids of Egypt and the spectacular palaces of Mesopotamia were built in countries whose civilization depended upon great rivers; in China there were the Great Wall and the enormous tomb which Ch'in Shih Huang Ti built for himself in the second century B.C. The scale of the Forbidden City in Peking, although built much later, reflects this monumental approach to architecture. It would be hard to think of anything in Europe or North America—where civilization depended on rainfall, not on mobilizing great numbers of men to control their water supplies—which breathes quite the same feeling of space and of immensity.

The Hsia Dynasty may or may not have existed. There was very likely a comparatively small state of

Hsia, and its people may have been those who produced either the Painted or the Black Pottery of Neolithic times. But we do not know.

The Hsia were supposedly succeeded by the Shang Dynasty about 1523 B.C., and until forty or fifty years ago historians were inclined to treat both as legendary. Recently, however, the existence of the Shang people has been proved beyond all doubt.

Near the city of Anyang, north of the Yellow River, is a district called the Waste of Yin, which was long rumored to be the site of the capital of the Shang Dynasty (Yin was the name given to the dynasty by its successors). Farmers plowing there kept turning up odd bones, polished smooth, with T-shaped cracks and occasionally with what looked like a curious form of writing. These, they concluded, must be the bones of dragons. And since "dragon bones" are highly prized in Chinese medicine, the more enterprising farmers sold the bones to doctors and chemists, who ground them up and prescribed small doses for their patients.

About the beginning of this century Chinese scholars came across some of these bones and realized that the odd markings were writing of a more archaic form than any yet known, but recognizably Chinese. With this began one of the most extraordinary archaeological discoveries in history.

The bones (usually leg bones of cattle, split, or tortoise shells) were Oracle Bones which had been used during the Shang Dynasty in divination by fire. When exposed to heat, the bone cracked, and the length and direction of the crack were interpreted to give an answer to whatever question the diviner was asking. It is a common enough way of divining in primitive cultures, and the Mongols still use the shoulder blade of a sheep for the same purpose, but what made these bones so valuable was that the questions, and sometimes the answers too, were inscribed on the bone. From them it was possible to learn how the people lived, how they built their houses, what crops they planted, and what animals they kept.

The bones are often more accurate than other records. Histories written after the event may reflect the prejudices of the writer. Ceremonial bronzes cast to commemorate a victory may double or treble the number of men involved. But a question put to the gods, and its supposed answer, are likely to be the simple truth.

What sort of questions did the people of Shang ask? They asked about the weather, especially rain; about the prospects for their crops of wheat and millet and for the liquor (probably something like beer) that they made from the millet. They asked when to attack their enemies and when to stay on the defensive; whether they would recover from an illness; and when to start out on a journey.

These were special questions. The Oracle Bones were probably also consulted regularly every ten days to discover whether the next ten-day period would be lucky or unlucky. The Shang calendar was based on a ten-day unit, with three units for a month and thirty-six units for a year. Extra ten-day units were added when necessary to keep this lunar calendar of three hundred and sixty days in line with the solar year of 365¼ days. (This Shang calendar was adjusted in later centuries, but its basic principles have remained the same throughout Chinese history.)

The finding of the Oracle Bones led to extensive excavations at the Waste of Yin, which did prove to be the site of the Great City Shang, last of the several capitals of the Shang-Yin Dynasty. And, in spite of the efforts of grave robbers, both ancient and modern, the great underground tombs discovered there yielded a wealth of information and treasure. They brought to light bronze vessels, marble sculpture, and fine white pottery; daggers, ornaments, and chariot fittings; musical instruments; jade, ivory, and inlaid bone.

Above all they showed how much that has been characteristic of Chinese life through the centuries—ancestor worship, the solidarity of the family, the calendar (all-important in an agricultural society), even the shape of vases and sacrificial vessels—was already established in the second millennium B.C. The houses built then were built on the plan used in Chinese houses to this day: a peaked roof supported by rows of pillars, the walls—whether of pounded earth as they were then, or of brick as they usually are now—being incidental and not used to support the roof. The city was almost certainly walled.

From the writing on the Oracle Bones it is clear that the Chinese language was already well formed. This is important because, although every country's language is a major element in its culture, the Chinese language played perhaps a greater part than any other. It is quite different from the Western or Indo-European languages. It is uninflected—that is, it does not have special endings for the plural or for tenses—and it is written not in a phonetic script but in ideograms. Like Egyptian hieroglyphics, Chinese writing started with pictographs, but whereas the Western languages soon moved on to phonetic scripts, the uninflected nature of Chinese made such a script unnecessary; instead the Chinese developed their system of characters.

Some characters still reveal their pictorial origin. For example, 日 (originally ⊖) means the sun; 月 (which was originally ) means the moon; 木, a tree, was first written 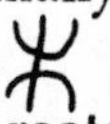, the top being the branches and the bottom the roots. These were then developed in various ways: the sun and the moon were put together to mean brightness (明); a woman (女) under a roof (宀) became 安, meaning peace; a woman beside a child (好) means good.

This, of course, is not the whole story. The development of the Chinese language is an enormously complicated study which we cannot go into here, but two points should be mentioned.

The first is that because Chinese characters carry their meaning in themselves, virtually independent of pronunciation, they enable people who speak quite different languages to communicate with each other. The languages spoken in north and south China are as different as Swedish, say, is from German. But only one written language is needed. The written Chinese language was therefore of great importance in pulling China together as a nation. It also brought non-Chinese races under Chinese cultural influence. When the Japanese decided, at the beginning of the fifth century A.D., that they must have a written language, they took over the Chinese script lock, stock, and barrel, so that even today an educated Japanese can read Chinese without being able to speak a word of it. The same thing happened to the Koreans and the Vietnamese.

The second point is that Chinese characters were

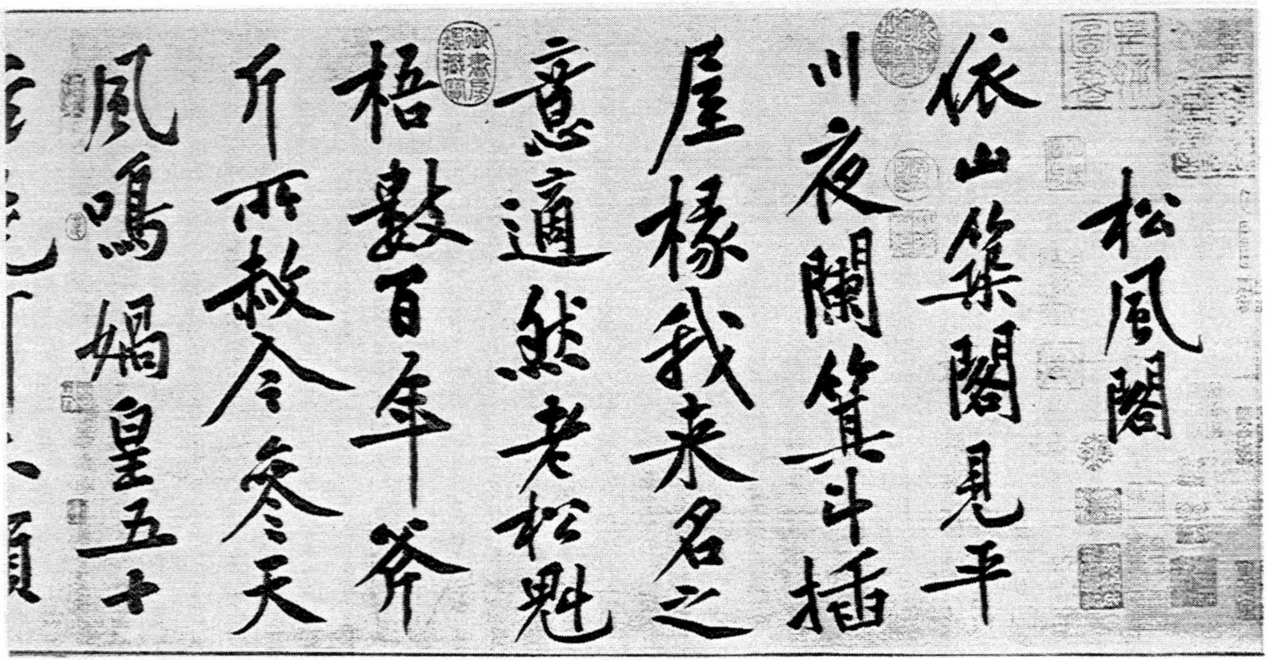

Detail from "The Hall of Pines and Wind." An example of calligraphy by Huang T'ing-chien (Sung Dynasty)—*Collection of the National Palace Museum, Taipei, Taiwan, Republic of China*

drawn with a brush, using much the same technique as in painting. Writing brushes may have been in use as early as the Shang Dynasty. Chinese characters and handwriting came to be prized as works of art in themselves, and this had an immense influence on the styles of Chinese painting.

All the evidence from Anyang thus suggests that the Shang Dynasty had achieved a remarkable and unmistakably Chinese culture. In one form of art it was superior to anything that followed: that is, the casting of bronze. It is possible that the fundamental techniques of casting may have reached China from the West, but there is no proof of this. The earliest Shang bronzes yet discovered are completely Chinese in style as well as highly skilled in execution. In fact, Shang bronzes

Bronze wine vessel in the shape of an owl (Shang-Yin Dynasty; about 1523–1027 B.C.)—*Courtesy, the Trustees of the British Museum, London*

are thought by some to be not only finer than anything produced later in China but also finer than the best work of the Renaissance. The designs, too, have a vigor and a vitality rarely if ever equaled elsewhere.

Until the discovery of the Great City Shang, foreign experts were inclined to attribute the best bronzes, of the type claimed by the Chinese to be Shang, to the latter part of the succeeding Chou Dynasty. It was hard to believe that they could be earlier. Now it seems that the Chinese themselves, far from inventing the Shang-Yin Dynasty, have done it less than justice.

2

The Mandate of Heaven

"Wen and Wu received the Decree of Heaven."
(Inscription on a bronze of the Chou Dynasty)

THE OVERTHROW of the Shang Dynasty in the second millennium B.C. appears in the records of the victorious Chou Dynasty as a simple matter of good and evil. The first two kings of Chou, Wen Wang and his son Wu Wang, embody every virtue; they are brave, compassionate, and loyal. The Duke of Chou, a younger son of Wen Wang, who played a great part in the conquest of Shang and the consolidation of the new empire, excelled even these two paragons. Centuries later Wen Wang and the Duke of Chou were to become the ideal heroes of Confucius.

The founders of Chou being so virtuous, they would not have raised their hand against their king unless Heaven willed it. Thus was born the doctrine of the Mandate of Heaven: the belief that a sovereign ruled only with the approval of Heaven, which might be withdrawn, and that a man of exceptional virtue might be chosen by Heaven to ascend the throne even against his will. A ruler was also held responsible for everything that happened during his reign: for floods, famine, earthquakes, and all natural disasters as well as for civil war; and for the harvest, whether good or bad; all this depended upon his virtue.

The success of this doctrine must be the envy of all

propagandists. For three thousand years the idea of the Mandate of Heaven has been accepted by its victims as well as by those who profited from it. The responsibility was overwhelming. In times of drought or flood, conscientious emperors would implore Heaven to tell them what they had done wrong, never doubting that they were responsible for the catastrophe; others went to the opposite extreme and abandoned themselves hopelessly to the pleasures of harem and palace.

The doctrine could not be proved wrong. A rebel against the throne would claim that the sovereign had lost Heaven's mandate, and if the rebellion succeeded the claim had to be true. Obviously, then, Chou Hsin, the last ruler of the Shang Dynasty, must have been unfit to rule. Ssu-ma Ch'ien, who, at the beginning of the first century B.C., wrote the earliest comprehensive history of China, described Chou Hsin as a "man of quick discernment, gifted with sharp senses, mental ability beyond the ordinary, and physical strength of brutal power. . . . He loved the pleasures of the cup and debauchery, and was infatuated with his consort, the beloved Ta Chi, whose words he obeyed."

The details of his crimes, as recorded in other histories, suggest that Chou Hsin was really too wicked to be true. A typical example, one which particularly horrified the Chinese, because of their respect for age and family, is the story of how an uncle of Chou Hsin reproached him for his cruelty, and the sovereign replied: "My uncle is a wise man. It is said that the heart of a wise man has seven openings. Let us find out whether this is so!" The unfortunate uncle was killed on the spot, and Chou Hsin himself cut out his heart.

Ta Chi, his evil queen, was said not to have been a

woman at all, but a female demon, her true nature being revealed by the fact that she had goats' hoofs. She kept these bound with ribbons, a habit which supposedly gave rise to the exceedingly painful custom of binding girls' feet, a custom practiced well into the twentieth century. (Bound feet, however, did not actually come into fashion until some two thousand years after Ta Chi.)

Chou Hsin's capital, the supposed setting of his unspeakable crimes, was that same Great City Shang whose existence has been so abundantly proved by excavations at the Waste of Yin. No evidence of his tyranny or his cruelty has been found there, and it seems likely that he was overthrown simply because Wen Wang and Wu Wang had more soldiers than he had.

The rulers of Chou—Wen Wang, Wu Wang, and their ancestors—came from the west, from the frontier regions. Exposed to pressure from nomad tribes in the west and north, they were probably tougher, less civilized, and more adventurous than the Shang. It was a pattern that would be repeated often again: a vassal state, defending the northwest frontier, would grow more powerful than the central government and, moving east, would overthrow it, only to weaken and be overthrown in its turn some centuries later.

A look at the map will show how the two principal capitals of ancient China fitted into this pattern. One is Ch'ang-an, modern Hsian, capital of Shensi Province. This lies in the basin of the Wei River, a little west of where it joins the Yellow River, and is surrounded by mountains which make it a natural fortress. It is also a strategic position of great importance, lying between the central plains of China and the route west into central Asia. There, within a few miles of each other, were the first capitals of the Chou Dynasty, of the Ch'in Dynasty which succeeded it, and the Han, the Sui, and the T'ang.

Some two hundred miles east is Lo-yang, often known as the Eastern Capital. It is in open, more prosperous country, less easily defended. Toward the middle or end of almost every early dynasty, the Chou, the Han, the Sui, and the T'ang in turn moved east to Lo-yang. In every case the move was a sign of weakness. It usually meant that they had left some vassal prince to defend their rear—that is, the strategic Western Capital at Ch'ang-an—and that he had built up a strong kingdom of his own.

The Chou Dynasty was probably founded about 1027 B.C. Its government was feudal, although the word may be misleading in relation to Western history. The king was, in theory, the absolute owner of the earth and all its people. He ruled, however, through vassals of varying rank, governing areas of various size, and these were sometimes powerful enough to threaten his authority. Toward the end of the Chou Dynasty their struggles for power became full-scale wars between independent states, and no one paid anything but lip service to the divine, "all-powerful" king. (The titles "Emperor" and "Son of Heaven" did not come into use until the following dynasty.)

Already, three thousand years ago, Chinese bureaucracy was well established. The duties laid down for the Six Ministries of Chou give some idea how detailed the administration was, and also what life in the capital must have been like.

The First Ministry governed the palace and the harem, or Inner Courts, providing for one royal consort, three wives of the second rank, nine wives of the third, twenty-seven of the fourth, and eighty-one of the fifth rank, plus girls and serving women. It was responsible for the workshops of weavers, tailors, shoemakers, and so forth; for cooks, butchers, and other servants; for furnishing, lighting, and heating the royal apartments and baths; for the ice-houses in which meat, when not smoked or preserved in vinegar, was kept fresh through the summer; for supplies of food and of fermented drinks made from millet and rice (tea was not yet known). This ministry was also responsible for doctors working in the palace. The doctors had to average at least six cures out of every ten patients, for it was said with some reason that, since fifty percent would recover anyway, a doctor who cured only half his patients was useless.

Most important, perhaps, the First Ministry dealt with money matters, and with all the records of the court. The officials who had charge of these became known as *Ju*, or "Gentlemen with Side-whiskers," because they liked to wear long, thin locks of hair on both cheeks. This habit became so identified with this particular class of scholars that in later times they made a point of carrying a miniature comb specially designed for their side-whiskers. The Ju are often called "literati," but not all of the literary class were Ju; they are also called Confucianists, and Confucius was indeed largely responsible for the survival of the Ju system, but they already existed before Confucius. We shall meet them again.

The Second Ministry directed labor, kept lists of the men, animals, and natural resources of the kingdom, and was also in charge of mining, agriculture, and the public granaries, which were supposed to keep a reserve stock equal to ten years' harvest. In theory, at least, this ministry controlled the actions of every member of society to such an extent that it even laid down the age of marriage. A man should be married before thirty, a girl before twenty, and anyone who died unmarried was to be buried outside the family graveyard, being considered an outcast from society.

Although the Second Ministry was responsible for rescuing the sun and moon from the monster that tried to devour them during eclipses, astronomers and astrologers came under the Third Ministry; so did fortune-tellers, musicians, and dancers. The Fourth Ministry dealt with war and the army but its Grand Marshal had several additional duties, such as regulating the hours of day and night by means of a water clock. The Fifth and Sixth Ministries were devoted to justice and public works respectively.

By the beginning of the eighth century B.C., the Chou Dynasty, having occupied the throne for nearly three hundred years, was in decline. A breaking point came when one of the rulers, Yu Wang by name, degraded his queen and their son, the heir apparent, for the sake of a beautiful concubine, and the heir apparent took refuge in one of the northwestern states. This incident provides the first definite date in Chinese history relative to the Western calendar. An ode written at the time spoke of the very heavens as being outraged by the king's behavior—

> "The sun and moon announce evil,
> Not keeping to their proper paths. . . ."

—and mentioned an eclipse of the sun which is known to have taken place in August, 776 B.C.

The deposed heir apparent allied himself with one of the northern "barbarian" tribes and marched against the Chou capital. In the ensuing battle Yu Wang was defeated and killed, and the city was destroyed. His son soon discovered, however, as other Chinese leaders were to do when they turned outside the Middle Kingdom (as China was called because it was considered the center of the world) for help, that he had "brought in lions to rid himself of dogs," for his allies had no intention of retiring again to their deserts.

With the help of several strong vassal states they were eventually pushed back, but even so the new ruler retreated east and built his capital at Lo-yang, thinking to be safer there. He was right, so long as the frontier behind him was securely held. As we have seen, this move from west to east was to become the classic pattern that would lead to a change of dynasty.

The Prince of Ch'in now took over the greater part of the original Chou lands, including that strategic area where the Wei River joins the Huang Ho, and acted as a buffer against the barbarians. A few centuries later Ch'in was to conquer the entire country.

After the move eastward the Chou kings, although maintaining their status as divine rulers, had very little power. The Middle Kingdom broke up into independent states, varying in number, which struggled against one another for five hundred years, forming alliances, expanding and contracting in a shifting kaleidoscope of power. The outlying states, especially, grew stronger, expanding at the expense of more primitive peoples, who were gradually absorbed into China and Chinese culture.

For an example of how power was lost and won, let

us look at the strange fortunes of Wu and Yüeh, the two leading states in southeast China in the fifth century B.C.

The King of Yüeh, one Kou Chien, gambled his entire strength in an attack on the capital of Wu, was overwhelmingly defeated, and was forced to sue for peace on any terms. The King of Wu might then have destroyed Yüeh. Instead, while annexing a large part of the rival state, he allowed Kou Chien to remain an independent ruler in what was left.

Far from being grateful, Kou Chien swore vengeance. He slept thereafter on a bed of logs, and daily drank a cup of gall to remind himself of his defeat. ("To sleep on firewood and taste gall" is an expression still used of someone bent on avenging a humiliating defeat. The Empress Dowager thus described her position in 1901 when she was forced to flee from Peking after the Boxer riots and the entry of foreign troops into the capital.) His austerity was not without humor, and once, when the people of a village presented him with a large jar of wine, Kou Chien carried it to the bank of a river nearby, which his troops were about to ford.

"How can I, who led my army to disgrace at the East Gate of Wu, enjoy what my men do not?" he said. "At least we shall all have a taste." And he emptied the wine into the water.

Kou Chien's objective was the destruction of Wu. Two individuals made this possible; both, in their way, typical of the Chinese scene in times of change and conflict. One was his chief adviser, Fan Li. The other was a girl, called Hsi Shih, whom Fan Li noticed one day washing raw silk on the banks of a river, and in whom he recognized a weapon more powerful than the armies of Yüeh or the austerities of its king.

Hsi Shih is said to have been the most beautiful woman in China's history, with a trick of frowning when worried which made her quite irresistible, and with a grace of movement not to be hidden by peasant clothes. Fan Li had her taught music, dancing, and other arts, and after three years he arranged for her to be introduced into the Inner Courts of Wu.

This move was brilliantly successful. The King of Wu fell madly in love with Hsi Shih, and soon lost interest in anything outside the walls of his harem. His army, his government, the affairs of state were all neglected while he entertained his beloved with music and poetry, with silks and jewels and out-of-season delicacies that went far to bankrupt the kingdom.

The end could be foreseen. The army of Yüeh invaded and conquered Wu, whereupon Kou Chien showed none of the generosity of his rival.

"Since Heaven has given me Wu, I dare not refuse it," he told the King of Wu. The latter thereupon committed suicide. The State of Wu ceased to exist in 473 B.C. and was never restored, although it is believed that some members of the royal family may have fled to Japan and settled there. As for Yüeh, it was swallowed up in its turn by a rival state in 334 B.C.

The fate of the adviser Fan Li provides a curious epilogue to the story. He accompanied Kou Chien when the latter rode north to announce his victory to the King of Chou, a formality which established his right to rule what he had already conquered. On the return journey, however, Fan Li disappeared one night, near the Five Lakes, leaving behind a note for one of his friends:

"When the bird is killed, one puts aside the bow; when the hare is taken, one eats the dog; when the enemy is defeated, one undoes the Minister to whom one owes the victory. This Count of Yüeh, with the long neck and the dark countenance, one can serve him in adversity but in good fortune he would be dangerous. Leave him, as I do!"

Poets in later years liked to fancy that Fan Li retired to a life of meditation: "Here among the mists and waters of the Five Lakes he tried to forget the world." Actually it seems that he went first to the State of Ch'i, where he became Chief Minister and built up a fortune. Still afraid of tempting fate, he resigned this office, gave away his money, and settled down under another name in yet another state. There he experimented with rearing fish in ponds, and rapidly acquired a third fortune. "To follow in the steps of him who crossed the Five Lakes" has come to mean winning fortune and fame.

3

Contending Schools of Thought

After the move to Lo-yang in 771 B.C., the Chou Dynasty survived until 256 B.C. These five centuries are divided roughly into two periods, the "Spring and Autumn" (from the title of a work by Confucius), from 722 to 481 B.C., and the "Warring States," from 481 to 221 B.C.

The difference between the two is one of increasing violence. During the Spring and Autumn period principles of legitimacy, and even chivalry, were accepted—at least in theory. The central states might be bitter rivals and were often at war, but they recognized each other's right to exist. There was almost a gentlemen's agreement that territorial expansion should be at the expense of barbarian or semi-barbarian tribes. The pastoral peoples of the north and west, and the mountain people of the south, originally non-Chinese in language and culture, were drawn, willingly or unwillingly, into the Middle Kingdom.

By the time of the Warring States these outlying regions had been largely absorbed. The older states no longer hesitated to destroy one another if they could. The change can be seen in the generous behavior of

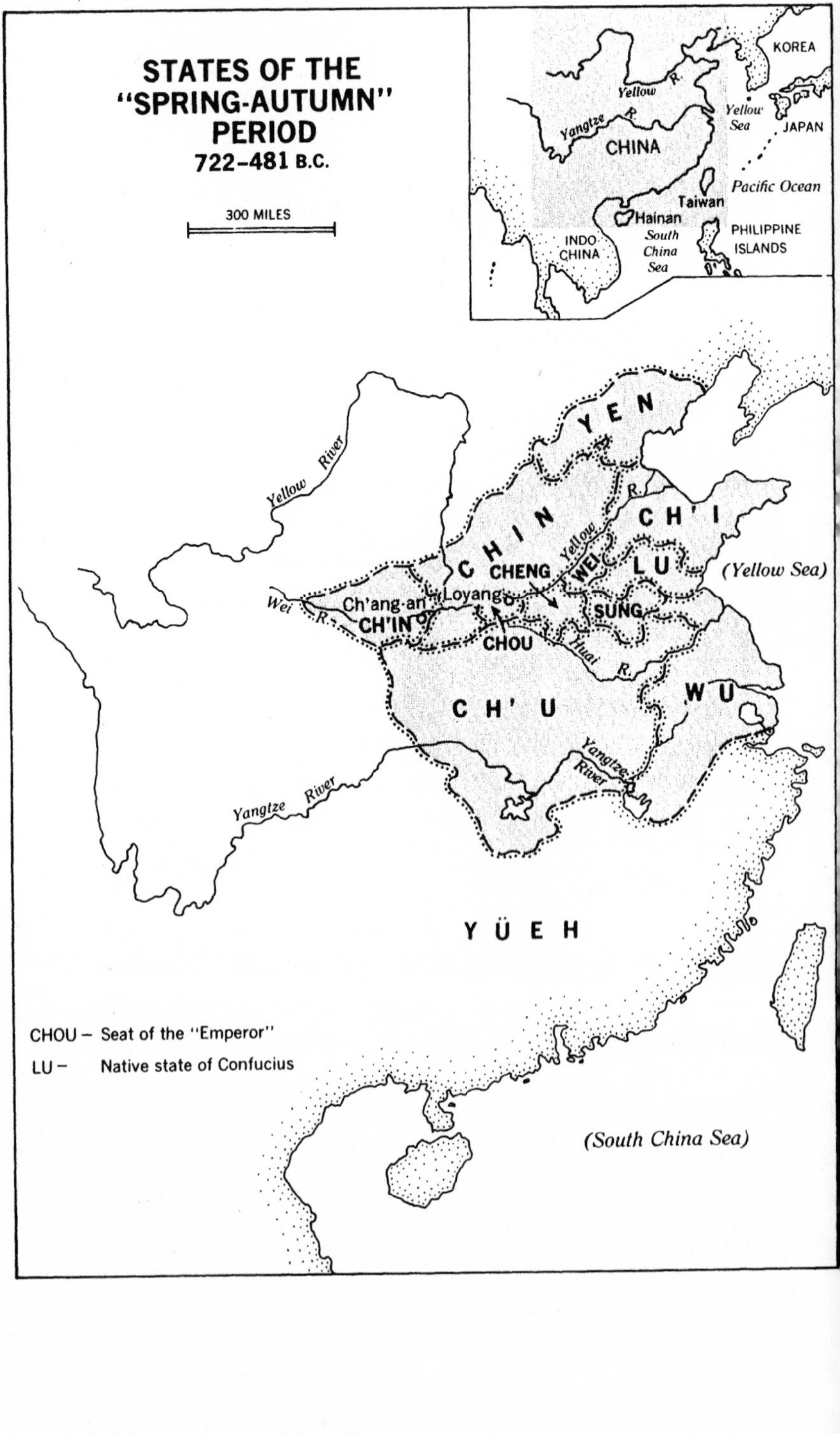
STATES OF THE
"SPRING-AUTUMN"
PERIOD
722–481 B.C.
300 MILES
KOREA
Yellow R.
Yangtze R.
CHINA
Yellow Sea
JAPAN
Pacific Ocean
Taiwan
Hainan
INDO-CHINA
South China Sea
PHILIPPINE ISLANDS
YEN
Yellow River
CHIN
CH'I
Yellow R.
CHENG
WEI
LU
(Yellow Sea)
Wei R.
Ch'ang-an
Loyang
CH'IN
SUNG
CHOU
Huai R.
CH'U
WU
Yangtze River
Yangtze River
YÜEH
CHOU – Seat of the "Emperor"
LU – Native state of Confucius
(South China Sea)

the King of Wu when he defeated Yüeh, and the King of Yüeh's annihilation of Wu when his turn came. Meanwhile the Kings of Chou were increasingly ignored for all but religious or ceremonial purposes, and leaders of several states openly took the title of *Wang*, or King, in defiance of Chou supremacy.

In the seventh century B.C. the state of Ch'i (roughly modern Shantung Province) suddenly took the lead under an enterprising ruler and his Chief Minister, who was known as Master Kuan. Master Kuan is credited with introducing, among other things, a new tax system, regular weights and measures, and a state monopoly of salt and iron. He was certainly a remarkable man—the first of a new type of statesmen who were to take the place of the feudal aristocrats and whose influence was to transform the Middle Kingdom.

The entire Eastern Chou period (i.e., after the move to Lo-yang) is notable for scholars, statesmen, and philosophers. These men wandered from one state to another in search of a ruler who would put their theories into practice, peddling ideas as traveling salesmen peddled their thread, or cloth, or pots and pans. They were often natives of the older, more conservative states, who, finding their ideas unwelcome there, made their way into the border states where life was more unsettled and they had a better chance of being listened to.

In the late 1950s, the Chinese Communists, trying to appear liberal, often referred to the "Hundred Schools" of thought: "Let a Hundred Flowers Bloom and a Hundred Schools contend." Under the Communists, this was a hollow mockery, but the Hundred Schools did exist. They were at their height between

500 and 250 B.C. They included Confucianists and Taoists, of course, while other schools ranged from the Mohists, with their doctrine of universal love, to the Legalists, who believed that man was basically evil and advocated rigid control and ruthless government.

This extraordinary burst of creative thought may have been due to the chaos of the times. There was no fixed pattern of life, no generally agreed form of government, and no powerful religious tradition. The ancient religion of China—in which the people worshiped local genii, including the spirits of their ancestors, while the Emperor, and only the Emperor, worshiped a single Supreme Being, the Sovereign on high—continued to be observed, but in these restless times it was not enough.

The Warring States were thus rivals in more ways than one: they fought with trade, with technological developments, and with ideas, as well as soldiers. An able man thought nothing of leaving his own state for another; and loyalty was given to an individual, enlightened prince rather than to Ch'i or Wu or Yüeh.

Academies of scholars were formed during the fourth century B.C., roughly contemporary with Plato's Academy at Athens. Increased, although indirect, communication through central Asia with the civilizations of India and the Mediterranean slowly brought in ideas from outside, and it is worth remembering that this classical age of China, this intense intellectual activity, coincided not only with the age of the Greek philosophers and the Hebrew prophets but with that of the Buddha in India. All the world seemed to be suddenly awakening.

Iron for weapons and for tools came into general use

during the Eastern Chou, as did chopsticks and copper coins. The first coins were made to resemble miniature knives, spades, or other familiar objects, but by the third century B.C. small round copper coins, with a square hole in the center (making them easy to string together) had become standard, and these continued to be made for over two thousand years. Lacquer was used at least as early as the fourth century B.C. The invention of the crossbow and the use of cavalry in place of war chariots made armies increasingly mobile, although the Chinese never equaled the northern nomads as horsemen.

Perhaps the greatest material advance was in agriculture. Increased irrigation, better use of the soil, and a new type of plow coincided with improved communications between one part of the country and another, which in turn made it easier to transport and store grain. The result, despite the turbulent times, was a steady growth in population: by the end of the Eastern Chou there may already have been more Chinese in the world than any other people. As the wealth of the country increased, so did literacy and education. This was yet another reason for the sudden outburst of new ideas: the old-fashioned, conservative statesmen were being challenged by men like Master Kuan of Ch'i.

Among the scholar-teachers of those centuries two stand out, their names familiar even in the West. (It is typical of China that neither is the original name.) Lao Tzu and Confucius were the founders of two of China's three religions (the third, Buddhism, came from India); and, although their philosophy as we know it now has been interpreted and reinterpreted by so many disciples that they themselves might not recognize it, Taoism and Confucianism have still to be taken into account in modern China.

They are poles apart. Taoism is an out-of-this-world religion—mystical, impracticable, much concerned with magic and immortality, teaching that men should look to their souls instead of trying to reform the world. "Do nothing and all things will be done!" (or, more accurately, "Do nothing, and nothing will not be done!") is one of the sayings most commonly credited to Lao Tzu. Rules, ceremonies, government, laws, and regulations are only necessary for those who have lost touch with nature.

Confucius, on the contrary, insisted that peace and order depended on every man's duty to every other man being regulated in detail, so that almost every word exchanged between ruler and subject, father and son, husband and wife, elder and younger brother, even friend and friend, should be according to rule. The perfect state left nothing to chance. Although Confucianism is in some sense a religion, its followers are preoccupied with this world and no other.

The contrast between Taoism and Confucianism is seen in the lives of the two philosophers. It is by no means certain that there was such a person as Lao Tzu. Although legends would have him living for five hundred years, or else born already old, with white hair, he was probably born about 604 B.C., and his surname is believed to have been Li. The historian Ssu-ma Ch'ien describes him as the Keeper of the Books at Lo-yang, the Chou capital. And in his old age he is said to have become so disillusioned by the violence of his times, and by the decline of the Chou Dynasty, that he de-

Portrait of Confucius (artist unknown)—*Collection of the National Palace Museum, Taipei, Taiwan, Republic of China*

Lao Tzu riding a water buffalo. Painting by Chang Lu (Ming Dynasty)—*Collection of the National Palace Museum, Taipei, Taiwan, Republic of China*

cided to leave the world and retire into the wilderness.

At Han-ku Pass, the boundary of Chou, the warden of the gate tried to persuade him to turn back and, when he refused, urged him at least to write down the essence of his philosophy for the generations to come. Moved by this appeal, Lao Tzu is said to have written five thousand characters there and then, trying to define the *Tao,* or "Way," which he had always before said it was impossible to describe. Then he went on his way to the west, riding a black buffalo, and was never heard of again.

The work supposedly written by Lao Tzu at Han-ku Pass, the *Tao Te Ching,* probably dates from the third or second century B.C., long after his time. Those who deny that it could have been written by the Master can quote his own words, neatly expressed by the poet Po Chü-i:

> " 'Who know, speak not; who speak, know naught'
> Are words from Lao Tzu's lore.
> What then becomes of Lao Tzu's own
> Five thousand words and more?"

Whoever its author, the *Tao Te Ching* provided the Taoists with a text that could be variously interpreted. The Taoist ideal is a world of natural harmony, undisturbed by human activities. There is neither good nor evil, beauty nor ugliness, except as introduced by man. Without wealth, there would be no thieves; without laws, no crime. Progress is to be avoided, knowledge is undesirable, and even such apparently useful inventions as writing, currency, and the wheel only add to the burdens of mankind.

Chuang-tzu, in the fourth century B.C., was perhaps

the greatest interpreter of Taoism. He especially enjoyed turning down offers of employment. It is said that once, when he was fishing, two officials from Ch'u came to invite him to become Chief Minister of their state, whereupon he replied:

"I hear that there is a sacred tortoise in Ch'u, dead three thousand years, and that your Prince keeps it on the altar in the ancestral temple. Now do you think that tortoise would rather be dead and venerated, or still alive and wagging its tail in the mud?"

"Alive and wagging its tail, by all means."

"Begone then, and let me wag my tail in the mud!"

Chuang-tzu was as otherworldly as Lao Tzu. Having dreamt one night that he was a butterfly, he said to his disciples next morning: "What is reality? Was I Chuang-tzu dreaming that I was a butterfly, or am I a butterfly now dreaming that I am Chuang-tzu?" When he was dying and his disciples spoke of funeral arrangements, the sage rebuked them. "With Heaven and earth as my coffin, the sun, the moon and the stars to attend me, and all creation escorting me to the grave—what else do I need?"

Ironically, in view of its scorn of material things, Taoism contributed much to Chinese medicine, science, and cooking. The Taoists were always seeking two things in this life: the elixir of immortality and the secret of turning base metal into gold. Their alchemists' experiments with zinc, copper, and lead, sulphur and arsenic, led to discoveries in chemistry and metallurgy, as well as such by-products as gunpowder, fireworks, and glazes for fine porcelain. Their sampling of almost everything edible (herbs, fungi, and the like) in their search for eternal life is probably one reason for the wonderful variety of the ingredients used in Chinese cooking. (There were, of course, casualties on the way: in the T'ang Dynasty alone three if not four emperors died of poisoning in their quest for immortality.)

Lao Tzu and Confucius are said to have met in Lo-yang in 517 B.C., when the former would have been about eighty-seven and the latter thirty-five. According to the Taoists, who probably invented this story, Lao Tzu lectured Confucius on the hopelessness of seeking the "Way" through good conduct or even in the world of men at all. And after the interview Confucius confessed that, although he understood how birds flew, how fish swam, how men and other animals lived, he could not hope to understand the flight of a dragon—and Lao Tzu was a dragon.

It is unlikely that Confucius was so modest. He was as convinced as Lao Tzu that his way was *the* way. His heroes were Wen Wang, Wu Wang, and the Duke of Chou, the three founders of the Chou Dynasty, and he believed in the Mandate of Heaven. Peace, prosperity, a good harvest, and a contented people were the natural results of a virtuous ruler.

Confucius was born in the state of Lu, or southern Shantung, about 551 B.C. He came of good family and, indeed, may have been descended from the kings of the Shang-Yin Dynasty. In his youth he held various minor offices, but by the age of twenty-two he had become a teacher, and he soon gathered around him a number of devoted disciples. His greatest interest even then was in the past. His visit to Lo-yang, when he was supposed to have met Lao Tzu, was in order to study the ceremonies and music of the early Chou Dynasty, which made a great impression upon him.

About 500 B.C. he agreed to take office in Lu, and it is said that for a time the Duke of Lu followed his advice in everything. The state enjoyed prosperity and peace. This was, however, too good to last. The duke of a neighboring state, alarmed at the increasing power of Lu, sent a gift of eighty beautiful girls and a hundred and twenty horses to the Duke of Lu; he hoped, quite correctly as it turned out, that the latter would be so delighted by these that he would forget the wise principles of Confucius.

In 495 B.C., therefore, the Master (K'ung Fu-tzu, from which we get Confucius, means Master K'ung, his personal name being K'ung Ch'iu) resigned and went into exile. For thirteen years he traveled from one state to another, followed by a few faithful disciples, in search of a ruler who would be guided by his theories. He did not return to his native Lu until he was an old man, a few years before he died. Meanwhile some of the princes he visited received him with honor and listened politely to his teachings, but others ignored him. None were prepared to let him reform their government.

During his wanderings Confucius collected and edited a number of historical records, and after his return to Lu he wrote his only original work: the *Spring and Autumn Annals,* a history of Lu from 722 B.C. to his own time. His philosophy, however, is best known from the *Analects,* which were written down later by his disciples, and which give his answers to questions, usually beginning with the words "The Master said . . ."

In the spring of 481 B.C. the Duke of Lu captured a curious animal while out hunting one day, and Confucius was called upon to identify it. He recognized the

Ch'i-lin, a supernatural creature with a single horn which is sometimes identified with the unicorn. Its appearance was believed to foretell the death of a great man, and Confucius knew at once that it had come for him. "My work is at an end," he said, put aside his brush, and closed the *Spring and Autumn Annals* with the record of the Ch'i-lin's appearance.

He lived, however, another two years. Then early one morning a disciple heard him lamenting:

> "The great mountain must crumble;
> The strong beam must break;
> And the wise man wither away like a plant."

The disciple hurried to his side. "My time has come to die," Confucius told him. "No intelligent monarch arises; there is not one in the kingdom that will make me his master."

Thus described, the end of his life may seem sad. Yet he never lost confidence. One feels that he would not have been in the least surprised to find that his philosophy became the strongest single influence in Chinese life for more than two thousand years.

Confucius' teachings were conservative. He did not question that men were born into their proper station in life: "Let the ruler be a ruler and the subject a subject; let the father be a father and the son a son." He did not look beyond the known world and, when questioned about death, he replied that, since man did not yet understand life, how could he hope to understand death?

He was nevertheless, in his own way, a revolutionary. Princes were born to rule, yes, but the wise man was born to instruct the prince, and it was the duty of the ruler to obey. Might was by no means right; no man, emperor or slave, was above moral law. "Confucius was China's first great moralist," as John K. Fairbank points out, "the founder of a great ethical tradition in a civilization which above all others came to concentrate on ethical values."

His ideal, the Superior Man, possessed definite virtues: loyalty, integrity, humanity. To these he added *li,* which means "ritual," but to which he gave a much wider interpretation. *Li* is a way of doing things, of politeness, of etiquette in the sense of smoothing the rough edges of behavior, a feeling that inner virtue expresses itself in a code of manners—almost, indeed, that if you observe the code the virtue will follow.

Much of Confucian philosophy is to be found in the "Five Classics" of ancient China. These are: the *Spring and Autumn Annals,* written by the Master; the *Book of History* and the *Book of Poetry,* believed to have been collected and edited by him; the *I Li,* or *Classic of Rituals,* and the *I Ching,* or *Classic of Changes.* The last, a somewhat incomprehensible work of symbolism and mysticism, is based on eight famous trigrams of whole and broken lines called the Pa Kua. The Pa Kua are said to have been invented by the

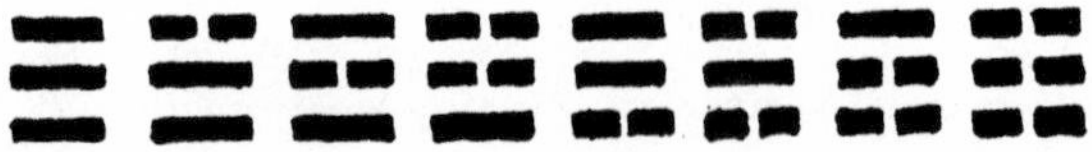

Pa Kua

legendary Emperor Fu Hsi, inspired by the markings on the back of a tortoise, and they may be meant to imitate the cracks on the tortoise shells that were used for divination. They can be interpreted in many different ways and are believed to provide a key to all the secrets of nature.

These whole and broken lines of the Pa Kua are also symbols of the masculine and feminine principles, called Yang and Yin. Yang represents heaven, light, and whatever is masculine and positive in character; Yin represents earth, darkness, and the feminine principle. Together they form what is probably the oldest symbol in the world:

Yin and Yang

This shows how day and night, man and woman, heaven and earth, complement each other and together make up a perfect whole.

The *I Ching*, incidentally, gives the oldest known example of a magic square, in which the numbers total the same when added in any direction. The black circles are even numbers, and feminine; the white are odd, and masculine. Thus the square becomes:

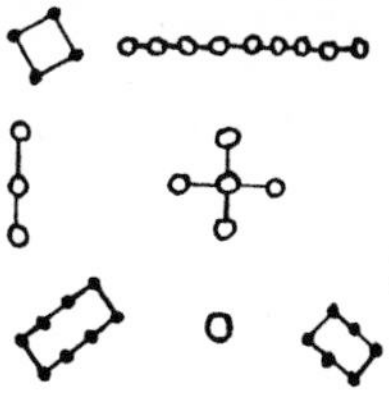

4	9	2
3	5	7
8	1	6

Magic squares

All of this takes us rather far from Confucius. The Master's teachings were carried on by his disciples, although the greatest of these—Meng Tzu, known to us as Mencius—was not born until more than a century after Confucius' death. His career echoed that of Confucius, and he too wandered from state to state without ever finding a prince who would put his preachings into practice. It was to be another two hundred years before the first emperor of the Han Dynasty deliberately adopted Confucian principles as the basis of his government.

4

Ch'in Shih Huang Ti, the First Universal Emperor

WE HAVE SEEN that, when the Chou Dynasty moved to Lo-yang in 771 B.C., the Prince of Ch'in took over the land along the strategic Wei valley, where the former capital had stood. This was the beginning of Ch'in's rise to power, and one of its main causes. Being a frontier state, it had to maintain a strong standing army, for at this time pressure from the nomad tribes to the north and west of China—those "barbarians" who were to play such an important part in her history—was increasing. To some extent Ch'in even adopted the weapons and the tactics of its "barbarian" neighbors. Yet at the same time the state was open to the vast range of new ideas suddenly springing to life in China.

Another reason for the growth of Ch'in was its willingness to make use of "foreigners" from other states. This was a deliberate policy, persisted in over the centuries in spite of opposition from native Ch'in statesmen. It was eloquently defended in 237 B.C. in a speech by the then Chief Minister Li Ssu, himself a foreigner. Addressing his ruler, he noted that he was wearing jade from the mountains of Kunlun and that pearls hung from his girdle.

"Your Majesty rides horses from the west," he went on. "He flies banners embroidered with green phoenixes, and listens to the beat of drums made from the skins of crocodiles. Yet Ch'in does not produce a single one of these treasures. . . .

"Why is T'ai-shan a great mountain? Because it uses every grain of sand, even the dust that blows upon it, to increase its stature. Why is the Huang Ho a great river; the sea so vast? Because they absorb every drop of water that reaches them."

The "foreigner" who contributed most to Ch'in was Lord Shang. He was a native of Wei who came over to Ch'in about 360 B.C., a century or more before Li Ssu, and he was a great believer in the Legalist school of thought: the theory that men must be governed by strict laws and severe punishments. His doctrines and his career were in striking contrast to those of Confucius. He had no regard for the past.

"It is the duty of the Superior Man to make new laws in every age," he said. "Some men, lacking in ability, may like to follow the old ways, but anyone who is able to introduce more efficient rules and regulations should not hesitate to do so."

Lord Shang did not hesitate. He transformed Ch'in from a feudal state into one with a powerful central administration, and he weakened the hereditary power of the princes by building up a new aristocracy among men, not of noble birth, who had distinguished themselves in government or in war. He also abolished the old system whereby agricultural land was divided into

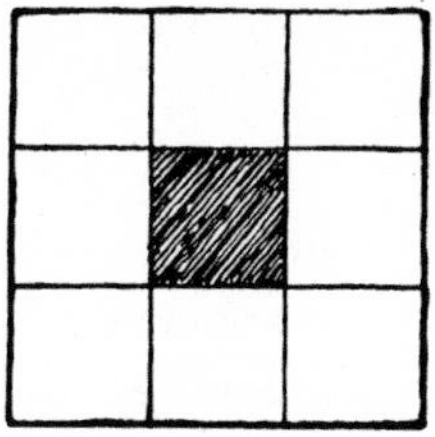

Division of agricultural land

units of nine fields and each unit was cultivated by eight families, with the government taking the produce of the ninth field as its share. Instead he introduced individual ownership of land, and direct taxation.

There are other policies of Lord Shang which have had a lasting influence on Chinese administration: for example, mutual responsibility. He divided the population of the state into groups of five or ten families, the members of which were supposed to help and support each other, but who were also required to denounce any one of their number who broke even the most trivial law. Otherwise, they were liable to the same punishment as the criminal. Carried to its logical conclusion, this meant that, when the heir apparent of Ch'in disobeyed the new laws, Lord Shang, unable to punish his master's son, ordered the chief royal tutor executed and the assistant royal tutor branded. There was no doubt that he meant what he said.

Lord Shang is also credited, rightly or wrongly, with introducing the barbarian custom of paying a premium for enemy heads after a battle. It is not surprising that other states of the Middle Kingdom now denounced Ch'in as a savage country, with the heart of a tiger.

Nevertheless, the policy of strict discipline, ruthlessness, and terror paid off. The people of Ch'in were law-abiding and industrious; its army was well-nigh invincible.

The great statesman fell victim to his own laws. His patron died, to be succeeded by that same prince whose tutors Lord Shang had dealt with so harshly; and he had to flee for his life. He tried to find shelter at a small inn, but the innkeeper pointed out that he could not allow anyone without an official identity card to stay at his inn; if he did, he was liable to the same penalty as the man he sheltered.

"Alas, that my own wise regulations should be turned against me!" cried Lord Shang. He fled again, but was captured after a brave stand on his own estates; his body was torn apart in the marketplace by five horses, and all of his family were executed.

The powerful state he had built survived him. One by one Ch'in defeated or absorbed others of the Warring States, and in 256 B.C. the Ch'in ruler overthrew the last King of Chou and occupied the Chou capital. Although it was another thirty-five years before Ch'in controlled the whole of China (the Ch'in Dynasty can therefore be dated from either 256 or 221 B.C.), there was no doubt thereafter that Ch'in had received the Mandate of Heaven.

The First Universal Emperor, as he named himself, was born Prince Cheng, and he came to the throne of Ch'in in 247 B.C. at the age of thirteen. He soon proved himself equal to the opportunity he had inherited, and after the final conquests in 221 B.C. he took the title of Ch'in Shih Huang Ti, or Ch'in First Sovereign-Divine-Ruler, and decreed that his successors should be known

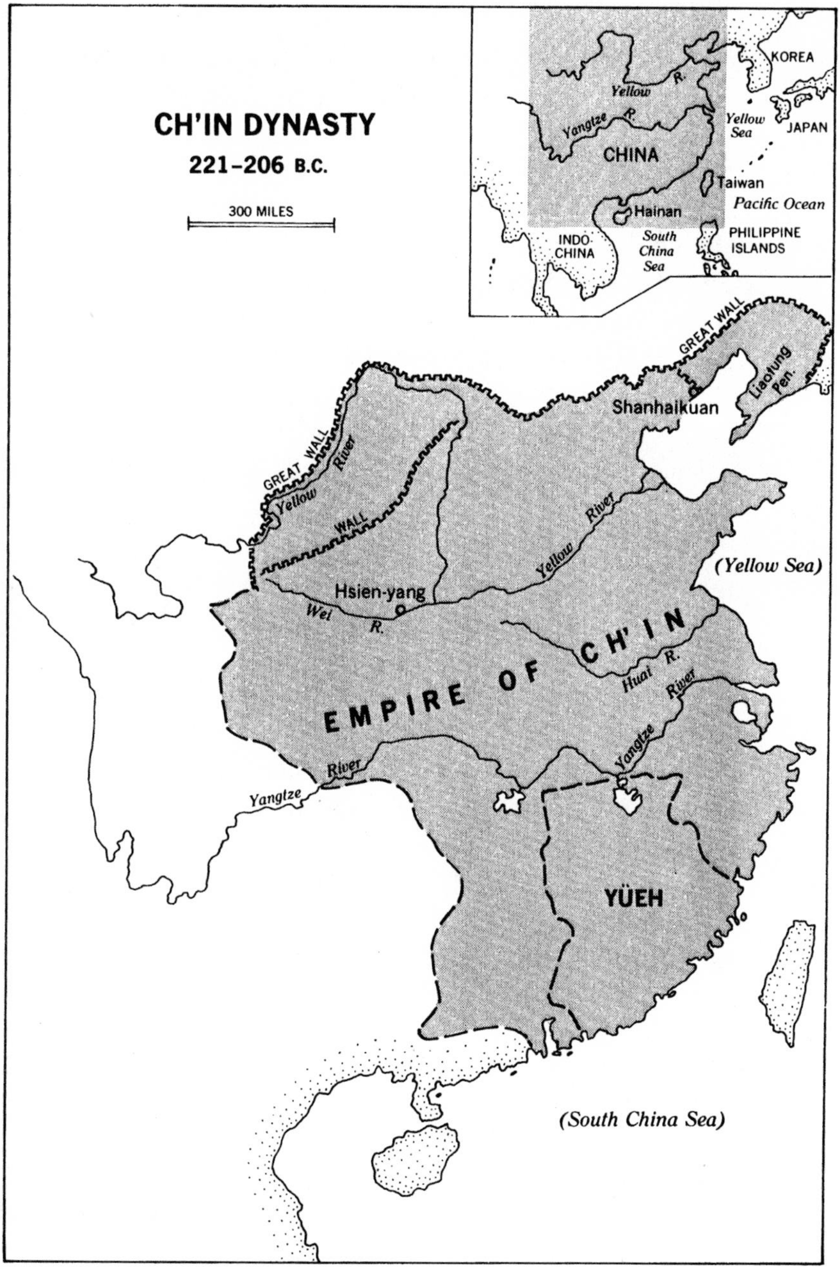

CH'IN DYNASTY
221–206 B.C.
300 MILES
KOREA
Yellow
R.
Yangtze
R.
Yellow Sea
JAPAN
CHINA
Taiwan
Pacific Ocean
Hainan
INDO-CHINA
South China Sea
PHILIPPINE ISLANDS
GREAT WALL
Liaotung Pen.
Shanhaikuan
GREAT WALL
Yellow
River
WALL
Yellow
River
(Yellow Sea)
Hsien-yang
Wei
R.
EMPIRE OF CH'IN
Huai
R.
Yangtze
River
River
Yangtze
YÜEH
(South China Sea)

as Ch'in Second, Ch'in Third Sovereign-Divine-Ruler, and so on to the ten-thousandth generation.

It is not going too far to say that Shih Huang Ti created China. Earlier kings had ruled loosely over a feudal society, or over one of several states. After Shih Huang Ti, although there were civil wars, and the country several times broke up into independent kingdoms, the idea of a single supreme ruler and a central government survived. China was a nation. It also began to assume more or less its present shape, expanding to the south, for Ch'in Shih Huang Ti founded military colonies in an area corresponding roughly to modern Kwangtung Province, with parts of Kwangsi.

Even the name by which we know the Middle Kingdom came from Ch'in. The ships of Ch'in Shih Huang Ti sailed as far as India; and the Indians, and through them the Persians, Egyptians, and other western peoples, took the name of the ruling dynasty as the name of the land.

The historian Ssu-ma Ch'ien described Ch'in Shih Huang Ti as having "a high-pointed nose, slit eyes, pigeon breast, wolf voice, tiger heart." He was ruthless, extravagant, somewhat gullible in his later years, but undoubtedly a genius. He now carried out in the whole of China the reforms introduced by Lord Shang in the single state of Ch'in a century earlier. He was determined to have a united country. He refused absolutely to allow the rulers of the old states to retain any power, even as his vassals, but he also refused to replace them with his own relatives, saying that he had not overthrown one aristocracy only to substitute another of his own making. Instead, he ruthlessly carved the states up into provinces and districts which cut across their former boundaries, and he appointed viceroys to rule these for fixed periods. In theory, it was to be impossible ever to re-establish hereditary rule in the provinces, or to allow vassals to grow strong enough to challenge the Emperor.

Shih Huang Ti was one of the great builders of history. Roads, canals, and palaces were laid out on a scale never before imagined. Highways were built over hundreds of miles where there had never been more than a cart-track, and some of these were a hundred yards wide, with a central section ten yards wide reserved for the Emperor alone. (This is not unusual in Chinese architecture: imperial palaces have a central gate, a central flight of steps, and so on, used only by the Son of Heaven.)

These roads and canals were all centered on the Ch'in capital, Hsien-yang. Meanwhile all the most powerful families from the former states, said to have numbered over a hundred thousand, were ordered to move into the capital. These may have been hostages; more important, they concentrated the wealth of the entire country under the eye of its ruler. Making clear his own position as King of Kings, Shih Huang Ti also ordered an exact copy of the palace of every ruler he had defeated to be built in a park outside the city. These were furnished with dancing girls, musicians, servants, and cooks from the different states, so that if he wished to enjoy the pleasures of the former courts of Wei, or Yen, or Chao, he had only to visit them.

He built his own tomb at the foot of a mountain south of the capital. There, underground, he had a huge relief map of the Middle Kingdom done in bronze, the rivers and the sea filled with quicksilver—or so it is said, although the word used might mean "water like silver." The capital, with its palaces, buildings, and streets, was reproduced in miniature. Above all this the roof of the huge artificial cave was painted to represent the night sky and the stars.

Yet these were minor works. Ch'in Shih Huang Ti also built the Great Wall. Earlier walls had been built by several of the states, and cities were always walled, but now the Emperor conceived the idea of a single wall, incorporating the already existing state walls and completely separating what was China from what was not. He seems originally to have intended a horseshoe-shaped wall, open only to the sea. Later, however, he came to the conclusion that the natural barriers to the west and south of the country were so formidable that only the north needed to be protected.

In fact, until the coming of the Europeans by sea, it was only from the north that China was ever invaded. "Have no fear of the tiger from the south; beware the rooster from the north!" warns a Chinese proverb.

The Great Wall is a boundary between two geographically distinct areas, and until recently it marked the division between two different ways of life, that of the farmer and that of the shepherd.

As far back as we have any evidence, even when their homes were nothing more than shallow pits scraped out of the earth, the Chinese were a settled people. They lived from the soil—plowing, planting, reaping, and storing their crops from one year to the next—and they were deeply attached to their own plot of land, however small. As the country developed from individual states into a nation, expanded, and took on its present shape, the life of the ordinary farmer changed little, if at all. North of China proper, however, the climate was harsh, dry, and altogether unsuited to agriculture. The people were nomads, dependent on their flocks, and moving from one pasture to another at least twice a year.

We speak of nomads, or "barbarians," as the Chinese liked to call them. Who were these people? Originally they were probably of the same ethnic stock as the Chinese, developing along different lines because of geographic influences. They were by no means a single people, and through the centuries many different hordes came to power, dispersed, and reappeared under other names. They fought among themselves, or made alliances; disappeared like quicksilver, or suddenly found a leader such as Genghiz Khan and conquered half the world.

The first of the important nomad tribes were the Hsiung-nu, already menacing the northwest frontier when Ch'in Shih Huang Ti built the Great Wall; their power in Asia waned after the second century A.D., but they reappeared several centuries later in the west, where they were better known as the Huns. Among other tribes who rose and fell in the following centuries were the Hsien-pi, the Jou-Jan (nicknamed by the Chinese Juan-Juan, which means to wriggle or to crawl like worms), the T'u-chüeh, or Turks, and the Mongols. Further east there were Khitans, Juchens, and, much later, the Manchus, descendants of the Juchens. One of the Mongol tribes was called Ta-tar or Ta-tan by the Chinese, and this gave us the name Tartar, now often applied to all the northern nomads.

These people of the steppes were absolutely incomprehensible to the Chinese. It was not only that they lived in tents and wore rough clothes, drank mare's milk (no Chinese would drink the milk of any animal) or tea made from bricks of inferior tea leaves boiled for several hours, that they ate goat's cheese, and had no fuel for their fires except sheep and camel dung. It was that they did not even recognize the superiority of the Chinese way of life.

"If only they had a fraction of our needs, they would become our tributaries," one Chinese envoy to the Hsiung-nu complained. "But . . . we have sent them silk costumes; they have torn them to shreds hunting in thickets and then declared that silk was not as good as their sheepskins. We have sent them delicacies to eat; they have found them inferior to their milk and their koumiss [fermented mare's milk]."

Sometimes, over the centuries, tribes along the border tried to reconcile these opposing ways of life, but sooner or later they had to choose between a settled and a nomadic life,. The former usually won, for there was no doubt that Chinese culture was, in every material way, superior to that of the nomads.

In war, however, the nomads had three advantages: mobility, an understanding of horses, and great skill in archery. Their pasture-fed horses were far hardier than the stable-fed horses of the Chinese, and they themselves were so at home in the saddle that it was said their native country was the back of a horse. Finally, their extraordinary accuracy with bow and arrow, even at full gallop, made the nomadic mounted archer the most formidable soldier in Asia (as the English long-bow-man was the most formidable soldier in Europe) until the invention of firearms.

When China was weak, the nomads raided deep

into her territory and were gone before the defenders could mobilize. When China took the offensive, they simply vanished into the wilderness, and the Chinese might cover hundreds of miles of barren country without seeing a sign of life. Dependent upon a supply line, they had eventually to withdraw, whereupon the nomads trickled back into their old pastures. It was to put an end to this situation once and for all that Ch'in Shih Huang Ti determined to build the Great Wall.

Construction of the Wall started about 221 B.C., and it was virtually completed before Ch'in Shih Huang Ti died eleven years later. It remains one of the most astonishing structures in the world. The main wall is over 1,700 miles long, from the sea fortress at Shanhaikuan to the most western tower overlooking the deserts of central Asia, and, if you include inner and outer connecting walls, its length is more like 2,500 miles. It is said to be the only work of man which might be visible from the moon.

In the far west the Wall was either built of earth, moistened, pressed into shape with wooden forms, and thinly faced with stone, or it was built with layers of clay, beaten down hard, alternating with layers of brushwood or reeds, bound together in bundles eight feet long and eight inches thick, and laid crosswise. There it has inevitably been much eroded and worn away through the centuries. In the east, however, it was so solidly built that, although much restored by succeeding generations, the basic structure of the Wall we see today is that of Ch'in Shih Huang Ti.

The foundation, of granite blocks, was several feet deep. Bricks of baked clay were laid along both sides of this and cemented together, forming a solid outer

The Great Wall of China near Nan-K'ou Pass

shell almost two feet thick. The space between the two rows was then filled with hard-packed earth and rubble. The height of the Wall varied from fifteen to thirty feet, and its sides sloped inward from a twenty-five-foot base to a width of about fifteen feet at the top. On this was laid a stone causeway, wide enough for several horses to ride abreast, with a crenellated parapet along each side. Watch towers were built at intervals, close enough for smoke signals to be sent from each one to the next along its entire length.

What is most astonishing here in the east is not the size or the construction of the Great Wall, but the country across which it runs. Far from following the line of least resistance, it climbs over mountain ranges which no army could have crossed and plunges into valleys at an angle no horseman could have ridden. There is a legend that the bricks for building it were tied to the tails of mountain goats, as the only way of hauling them up the sheer heights, and in places it is hard to see how else they got there.

It could not have been done without enormous gangs of workmen and great human suffering. A million men are said to have worked on the Wall: convicts, criminals, local farmers rounded up against their will, even the princes of the conquered states; and so many died there that it earned the grim name of the Longest Cemetery in the World.

It was not for this, however, that Ch'in Shih Huang Ti was most hated. It was because of his quarrel with the scholar-official class—the Ju, or "Gentlemen with Side-whiskers"—a quarrel which resulted in the destruction of almost all the copies of the Classics and other historical works.

It was a quarrel which had long been brewing. Lord Shang seems to have already thought of outlawing the Classics a hundred and fifty years earlier, but he apparently realized that it could not be done until the country was united under one government. In the time of Ch'in Shih Huang Ti, therefore, the Ju were still an immensely powerful class. The administration depended upon them, and they were ready to oppose every move the Emperor made by quoting the Classics at him.

The climax came at a banquet one evening in 213 B.C., to which Shih Huang Ti had invited seventy of the principal Ju in an attempt to win them to his cause. In this he failed; the scholars continued to insist that "nothing can endure except those things in which we follow the example of antiquity."

Li Ssu, one of the great Legalists, thereupon seized the opportunity to present a plan for eliminating tradition and history once and for all. "Why should you, O Emperor, be forced to imitate men of the past?" he demanded. "The great rulers of antiquity each governed as he thought best at the time. These Ju praise what was only to discredit what is. They speak of an imaginary past only to cause trouble in the present. Now I, Li Ssu, suggest that all historical documents except the records of Ch'in be burnt . . . that whoever refers to the *Odes* and the *Annals* (the Books of Poetry and History) should be put to death, and his body displayed in the market place . . . that only works on medicine, divination, agriculture and gardening should be exempted, and that anyone who studies the past must do so at an officially approved school."

These suggestions were made law. Copies of the forbidden books were kept in the palace library, but otherwise the ban was complete. Anyone who was found with a copy of the Classics was branded and sent to work on the Great Wall. Four hundred and sixty scholars were executed (some say, buried alive) for continuing to teach the Classics. According to tradition, their mass grave so enriched the soil that melons grew there even in winter, whereas the site where the books were actually burned has remained barren from that day to this. And from that day to this Ch'in Shih Huang Ti's epitaph has been: "He burned the books and he buried the scholars!"

One should make clear, however, that the Emperor was not opposed to the Classics, or literature, as such; it was their use in the hands of the reactionary Ju. And it is hard to say how much, if anything, was permanently lost. Books were then written on bamboo tablets, bulky and difficult to hide. Moreover, the copies of the Classics preserved in the palace library were destroyed when the capital was sacked a few years after Shih Huang Ti's death. On the other hand, many scholars knew such works as the *Book of History* and the *Book of Poetry* by heart, and the ban against the books was officially repealed in 191 B.C., so that efforts were made to recover the missing books, or to rewrite them from memory, only a generation after they had been proscribed.

The effects of this attempt to destroy the past were nevertheless far-reaching. Some of the works supposedly recovered when the ban was lifted were almost certainly forgeries, and scholars have been arguing ever since about what is or is not genuine.

Ch'in Shih Huang Ti's achievements—the Great Wall, the canals, the roads, the palaces—were built at an enormous cost in human lives. The burning of the books turned the educated classes against him. Universally hated and feared, he narrowly escaped several attempts on his life, and toward the end of his reign he grew increasingly moody, suspicious, and superstitious. He hurried construction on the Wall because of a prophecy that "Hu" would destroy his empire, "Hu" being one of the names for the northern barbarians. He dreamed of immortality and became convinced that the Fountain of Youth was to be found on an island off the east coast of China. An expedition he sent out in search of this never returned, but it is possible that the ships reached Japan and that their crews were among the early colonists of that country.

The First Universal Emperor died in 210 B.C., aged fifty, while on a tour of the eastern provinces. His ministers, however, managed to conceal his death until they could get back to the capital. They announced that Shih Huang Ti was ill, pretending to serve him food, and to carry on conversations with him in his closed carriage. It was unfortunately midsummer, and the smell of the decaying corpse soon became noticeable, but the conspirators then ordered two cartloads of dried fish (a delicacy the Emperor was known to be very fond of) to be loaded on the carts accompanying the imperial carriage. The stink of fish overpowered any other odor.

Thus they reached the capital safely before announcing the Emperor's death. Nothing, however, could save the dynasty, and Ch'in survived the death of its founder by only a few years. The northern barbarians played no part in its downfall. Yet, in a sense, it could be said to have been destroyed by "Hu," as Ch'in Shih

Huang Ti had feared. The First Universal Emperor was succeeded by a worthless son, whose treachery and whose folly played a large part in the downfall of the dynasty, and who reigned only two years before being put to death by one of his own henchmen. His name was Hu Hai.

5

Liu Pang, Founder of the Han Dynasty

Ch'in Shih Huang Ti had destroyed Classical China. His achievements in uniting the country, in land reform, in government, in building, were prodigious, but they laid enormous burdens on the country. The First Emperor never won his people's support, and without that the Ch'in Dynasty could not survive.

The Han Dynasty succeeded where Ch'in had failed, building on its foundations—succeeded so well that ever since then the Chinese have been proud to call themselves Men of Han.

The founder of the dynasty, Liu Pang (later the Emperor Han Kao Tsu), was of peasant stock, a native of P'ei, in modern Kiangsu. He was not, and never became, a literary or well-educated man; he had none of the ruthlessness of Ch'in Shih Huang Ti, nor was he a great military strategist. But he had other qualities, among them honesty, shrewdness, an engaging disposition, and a quite extraordinary gift for leadership.

During the miserable last years before Shih Huang Ti's death, Liu Pang held some minor government post which involved his escorting gangs of convict laborers to work on the First Emperor's tomb. They knew, and he knew, that men assigned to such work were not likely to live long. One night, when he had stopped at an inn for a drink, he suddenly made up his mind.

"Gentlemen, all go away," he told the convicts. "From now on I am one of you."

From this beginning he became successively an outlaw, the leader of a band of rebels, self-proclaimed Duke of P'ei, and a general in one of the armies struggling for power after the death of Shih Huang Ti. In 206 B.C. he captured the Ch'in capital, and a grandson of Ch'in Shih Huang Ti—a nephew of the murdered Second Emperor, Hu Hai—surrendered the imperial seals of office to him. To everyone's surprise, he refused to allow his army to enter the city, and he would accept neither food nor other gifts from its people. He sealed up intact the palaces and treasuries of Ch'in. Then he ordered the complicated and tyrannical laws of Ch'in to be repealed immediately, replacing them with three simple rules for the punishment of murder, theft, and assault.

Liu Pang himself later dated his dynasty from this event. It was then he received the title King of Han. At that stage, however, he still recognized a prince of one of the old Warring States as his "Emperor," and he had also to reckon with the enmity of the other generals—in particular one Hsiang Yü, a giant of a man, ambitious, unscrupulous, and of violent temper. (Hsiang Yü's wife has become a symbol of self-sacrifice because, wishing him to be free to concentrate all his thoughts on the war, she killed herself and left instructions for her head to be sent to her husband; he wore it hanging at his belt for the rest of his life.)

Hsiang Yü now stormed down upon the Ch'in capital with his powerful army, and Liu Pang was forced to flee. The new conqueror thereupon turned his army loose in an orgy of looting and massacre. The city was burnt to the ground. This was the true, the final, "Burning of the Books," for the great imperial library, including the only surviving copies of many ancient works, was lost in the flames. Shih Huang Ti's mountain tomb, with its miniature world in bronze, its stores of gold and precious stones, was broken open, and the ashes of the First Universal Emperor were cast to the winds.

After another four years of bitter civil war, Hsiang Yü, whose ruthlessness had cost him many followers, was decisively defeated by Liu Pang. But the new Emperor faced enormous problems. China, so recently united, seemed about to break up again into the Warring States of the last few centuries. Dikes, roads, and canals were in disrepair. There were local rebellions everywhere, pockets of Ch'in resistance, and increasing threats from the Hsiung-nu, or Huns, in the north.

The Hsiung-nu reached the height of their power about this time, under the leadership of Modun (Chinese, Mao-tun), a heroic figure comparable to Genghiz Khan among the later Mongols. After a fiercely fought campaign, Modun routed the Yüeh-chih—one of the western hordes—so completely that the entire people, with their tents and their flocks, abandoned their own lands and migrated farther west. Modun celebrated his victory by making a silver-lined drinking cup out of the skull of the Yüeh-chih ruler. Then he turned his attention to China.

Liu Pang moved forces north to protect the frontier, and, underestimating the strength of the enemy, he himself rashly pushed ahead with a small advance party. He was immediately cut off and besieged in one of his own cities by Modun and 200,000 horsemen, and he only escaped capture because the Hsiung-nu withdrew as suddenly and as unaccountably as they had come, carrying away with them grain, cattle, and whatever else they could lay their hands on.

After this unfortunate episode Liu Pang concluded a treaty with the Hsiung-nu, giving them a yearly subsidy of brocaded robes, unspun silk for use in padded clothes, and wine, in exchange for their keeping the peace. He also presented Modun with a Chinese princess as his wife. At first he thought of sending his own daughter, in the hope that, if a son of hers eventually became ruler of the Hsiung-nu, they might be more amenable to Chinese influence; but, when the girl's mother protested, he chose one of the less attractive court ladies and represented her as his daughter. She was the first of many such "princesses" who were to suffer exile and the rough life of the nomads' tents, for it came to be taken for granted that every alliance would be cemented by the gift of a Chinese bride.

It was to be several years before the Han Dynasty was secure and a central government was firmly in control of the country. Liu Pang, however, laid the foundations for Han greatness from the very beginning, preserving the best of the Ch'in administration while making the laws less harsh, the taxes less exorbitant. He took what might be considered a backward step when he set up new vassal states, giving them considerable independence, but he soon recognized the dangers of this policy and decreed that the rulers of these states should always be members of the imperial family. (Later Han emperors further reduced their vassals' power by ordering that on the death of a vassal prince his lands must be divided among his sons, so that the great estates were constantly being split up.)

Liu Pang, now Emperor Kao Tsu, built his capital, Ch'ang-an (Everlasting Peace), on the Wei River near the ruined capital of the Ch'in, in the strategic heart of ancient China. It was on a scale suited to the ruler of "All under Heaven" (as the Chinese called the Middle Kingdom), and it was to become the most beautiful and most famous city in all Asia, but the Emperor, it is said, was shocked when he first saw the size of his own palace.

"The empire is scarcely won," he exclaimed. "What do we want with buildings like this?"

He hated the stiffness of court life. Never comfortable on the throne, he preferred to sit on the floor among his old comrades whenever he could. The old comrades, unfortunately, made themselves so much at home in the palace, drinking, quarreling, singing, and dancing, that they even tried to settle arguments about whose sword was the sharpest by slashing at the columns of the throne room. When court officials protested, the Emperor replied: "I won the world on horseback. Why should I bother about etiquette?"

"You won the world on horseback," his critic agreed, "but can you rule it from horseback?"

Being a man of common sense, Liu Pang reluctantly agreed that the court must observe some code of behavior. It was then that the preachings of Confucius at last came into their own. The Confucian scholars, despised and persecuted though they had been under Shih Huang Ti, were still influential; and, although Liu

Pang himself was not much interested in their theories, he did need educated and capable men, literary men, men who could help him administer the country, and by and large the Confucians were the men best qualified. Thus during the Han Dynasty Confucianism triumphed. From then until the beginning of this century it remained the accepted philosophy of the Chinese state, no matter what dynasty ruled.

In 195 B.C., some seven years after his formal accession to the throne, Liu Pang paid a visit to his native district, P'ei. More at home there than in the palaces of Ch'ang-an, he gathered the children around him and taught them songs, while at night he enjoyed the company of old friends, happily postponing his departure from one day to the next. One evening, during a feast, he accompanied himself on a five-stringed lute while he sang about the joy of returning to his own village after the conquest of the world. Yet he ended rather sadly:

> "How am I to find valiant men
> To defend the four quarters of the earth?"

On his way back to Ch'ang-an the Emperor was accidentally wounded by an arrow, and the wound would not heal. "Heaven decreed that I, a plain man, should become master of the world," he said, when the doctors admitted they could do nothing more. "Now Heaven will decide whether I live or die."

He died at Ch'ang-an in the summer of 195 B.C.

The Han Dynasty nearly died with its founder, from causes which were to recur often in Chinese history. Liu Pang was succeeded by his son, still a child, and the boy's mother became the real ruler of China. The

Empress Lü was a woman of strong character and had played a great part in her husband's success, but now she placed members of her own family in important positions, eliminating her rivals with extraordinary brutality, and finally established a dynasty of her own. It was not until after her death that loyalists succeeded in restoring the Han Dynasty.

Other empresses have usurped the throne of China, the most talented of these being the Empress Wu in the eighth century. The last was the Empress Dowager, who died only in 1908. Empress Lü, however, is the only one whose reign is considered legitimate by many historians, and she has been held up ever since as a terrible warning of the dangers of feminine rule. (Han Wu Ti avoided the risk of a young emperor's mother seizing power by naming his heir, and then ordering the boy's mother to commit suicide, but this solution was too drastic to be generally followed.)

The next half century was a time of consolidation. Then suddenly, under Emperor Han Wu Ti (141–87 B.C.), there was a burst of expansion, conquest, and exploration which transformed the Middle Kingdom into an empire comparable to that of Rome.

6

The Empire of Han

Wu Ti, a monarch of luxurious tastes, is often compared to Louis XIV of France. He was a poet, and his lament on the death of a favorite concubine has become famous:

"The sound of her silk skirt has stopped.
On the marble pavement dust grows.
Her empty room is cold and still.
Fallen leaves are piled against the doors.
Longing for that lovely lady
How can I bring my aching heart to rest?"

He was also a ruthless, ambitious ruler, determined that the power of the Han Dynasty should be unchallenged. He sent armies hundreds of thousands strong, one after another, into the northern deserts against the Hsiung-nu. Some never made contact with the enemy, some were wiped out, and all suffered heavy losses, but he did, gradually, and at a terrific cost in men and materials, destroy the menace of the barbarian hordes.

Many of the nomad tribes, especially those along the frontier, now became vassals of China. Some adopted Chinese ways, even building walls of their own against other tribes farther north. They formed a buffer zone, not unlike the barbarian auxiliaries of Rome, making it unnecessary for the Chinese themselves to maintain strong armies on the frontier—a sound policy, but one that had inevitably dangers of its own. Under a strong ruler the border tribes looked outward, defending their Chinese overlords; when China weakened, they were likely to turn inward. The "barbarian" conquerors of north China came, not from the outer steppes, but from the frontier tribes, semi-civilized by contact with the Middle Kingdom.

Part of Wu Ti's strategy against the Hsiung-nu was to prevent any alliance between them and the tribes on the Tibetan border, thus "cutting off the Tartar's right arm." He pushed the Great Wall still farther west; and, to make sure that the "Kansu Corridor" (so called because it later became a part of Kansu Province)—a panhandle of land stretching northwest from China proper into the deserts of central Asia—became a part of China, he settled several hundred thousand Chinese colonists there. Beyond this he built a string of fortresses, ruins of which remain, reaching far out across central Asia. Still he was not satisfied, not until he had made contact with the kingdoms which lay beyond those deserts.

Wu Ti hoped to find support in the west against the Hsiung-nu. He knew that when Modun had defeated the Yüeh-chih these had migrated westward and, although he had no idea how far they had gone, he determined to get in touch with them and to try to make them his allies. In 139 B.C. he sent one of his officers, Chang Ch'ien by name, in search of the missing tribe.

Chang Ch'ien set off with a hundred men, and the entire party was promptly captured by the Hsiung-nu.

They were held captive for ten years, during which time Chang Ch'ien married a woman of the Hsiung-nu and had children by her; but when, at last, he and a few of his companions managed to escape, they immediately continued their journey westward. After weeks of hardship and long marches they came to the kingdom of Ta Yuan, or Fergana (in Russian Turkistan), only to discover that the Yüeh-chih had migrated still farther, across the Pamir Mountains.

The King of Ta Yuan provided them with a guide, and when they finally reached the Yüeh-chih they were warmly welcomed. Although Chang Ch'ien did not succeed in forming an alliance with the tribe, who had no desire to be drawn back into the battles of east Asia, he stayed with them for over a year. He studied the geography and the customs, not only of the Yüeh-chih themselves, but of several neighboring kingdoms. He observed that the people of Ta Yuan, for instance, were farmers, like the Chinese, whereas the Yüeh-chih, the Wu-sun, and other tribes of western Asia were nomads, migrating with their flocks from season to season. He made note of crops foreign to China and brought back with him walnuts, alfalfa, the cultivated grape, and the art of making wine from grapes.

On his return journey Chang Ch'ien was again captured by the Hsiung-nu, but this time he escaped within a year, taking his wife and children with him. He reached Ch'ang-an in 126 B.C., after thirteen years, with only two of his original company.

Chang Ch'ien was one of the world's great explorers. The Chinese say that he "pierced the void," for he penetrated farther across central Asia than any single individual is known to have done before, and brought back

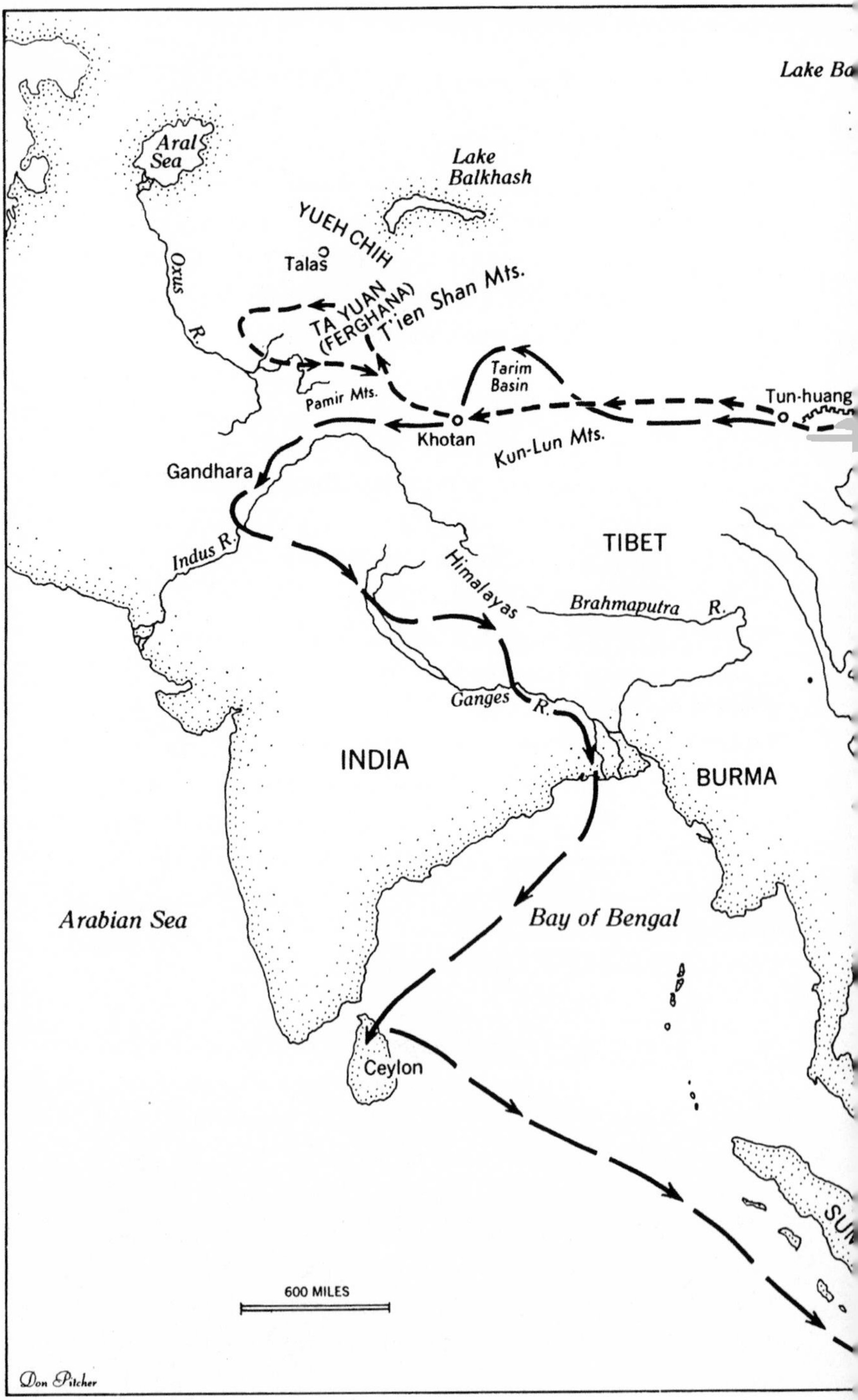
Lake Ba
Aral Sea
Lake Balkhash
YUEH CHIH
Talas
Oxus R.
TA YUAN (FERGHANA)
T'ien Shan Mts.
Tarim Basin
Tun-huang
Pamir Mts.
Khotan
Kun-Lun Mts.
Gandhara
TIBET
Indus R.
Himalayas
Brahmaputra R.
Ganges R.
INDIA
BURMA
Arabian Sea
Bay of Bengal
Ceylon
SUM
600 MILES
Don Pitcher

Amur River
Liao R.
Yalu R.
Sea of Japan
obi Desert
Tokyo
Pyong-yang
Kyoto
JAPAN
Seoul
Peking
KOREA
GREAT WALL
Yellow Sea
Yellow River
Loyang
Ch'ang-an
Shanghai
Nanking
River
CHINA
Taiwan
(Formosa)
Chang Ch'ien, 138-126 B.C.
Fa Hsien, 399-414 A.D.
Canton
Hainan
Philippine Islands
South China Sea
Pacific Ocean
-China
R.
BORNEO

knowledge of kingdoms whose existence had not even been suspected. Moreover, while he was among the Yüeh-chih, he found bamboo and cloth there which, he realized, must have come from south China, and he concluded that it might be possible to open up an overland route to the west by way of present-day Burma and India, thus avoiding the Hsiung-nu. The idea proved impracticable because of the great rivers and impenetrable jungles of that area, but it resulted in the exploration of the whole southwest. Chang Ch'ien himself made other expeditions, winning such a legendary reputation that he is even claimed to have sailed beyond the source of the Yellow River and found himself on the Milky Way—thus confirming what the Chinese had always believed, that the Huang Ho flows down from the "River of Heaven."

Chang Ch'ien's route to the west, the so-called "Silk Road," had in fact existed since time immemorial, but the number of different states and kingdoms along it, and their often unsettled political conditions, had meant that there was no direct contact between East and West. China and Europe remained ignorant of each other's existence. The route between them was like a chain, in which the separate links were only aware of a link or two on either side of them, having no idea of the length of the chain nor where it ended. Now, however, with the expanding empires of the Han Dynasty and of Rome at either end, it became possible to travel direct across central Asia. Chang Ch'ien's exploit thus led to a great increase in trade and in particular to the important silk trade with Rome which gave the road its name.

It also led to the curious episode of the Heavenly Horses. Chang Ch'ien reported that there was a breed of horse found in Ta Yuan which could cover three hundred miles a day, traveling full gallop over the roughest country, and which sweated blood. There was probably some truth in this. At a time when horses were either unshod or shod with leather and straw, mountain-bred horses would have been far superior to those bred on the plain; and as for "sweating blood," that may have been due to a tiny parasite known to afflict horses in that region.

Emperor Wu Ti in any case was determined to obtain these Heavenly Horses, as he called them, and he sent an embassy to the King of Ta Yuan offering in exchange a golden statue of a horse and a thousand ounces of gold. The King not only refused. He forbade his subjects to sell a single horse to the Chinese. When, in spite of this, they obtained a few and set off on their return journey, he sent troops after them to recapture the horses, whereupon the soldiers in their enthusiasm massacred the entire Chinese embassy.

Determined now to have not only his horses but revenge, Wu Ti sent one, and then another, army against Ta Yuan. The King refused to yield, and it was only when his own people rebelled, murdered him, and offered to supply the Chinese with all the horses they wanted that peace was finally made between them. Thirty Heavenly Horses, with three thousand of an inferior breed, were dispatched at once to the Emperor. Wu Ti was so delighted that he composed a hymn of welcome to the horses and wrote it out in his own handwriting.

These and other campaigns greatly impressed the kingdoms of the Western Regions. Many of their rulers sent gifts and hostages to the Chinese court, voluntarily recognizing Chinese suzerainty. By the end of Wu Ti's reign the Han empire in the west almost touched that of Rome.

Nor was the expansion of the empire confined to the west. In 108 B.C. Wu Ti invaded southern Manchuria and northern Korea and set up colonies there. In the south he established Chinese suzerainty, although somewhat loosely, over people who were racially and culturally different from the Chinese—people who were still hunters and fishermen, and who practiced only a primitive form of agriculture by clearing small areas from the forest just before the rainy season and planting crops there. Thereafter the Chinese written language and Chinese culture spread gradually southward into the Indochinese peninsula.

Wu Ti raised the money he needed for this expansion by introducing new taxes and by making the production of salt, iron, fermented drinks, and, above all, the minting of new coins, a government monopoly. He also indulged in more dubious practices, allowing certain titles to be sold and certain criminals to buy their freedom. And whenever his nobles came to pay court they had to present their seals of office to him on a piece of white deerskin—skin which could only be obtained, at an exorbitant price, from the imperial game reserves.

The Han Dynasty nevertheless achieved a remarkable balance, economically, and in government. China was already developing an efficient civil service, based on education and merit, far in advance of the West. Moreover, the two apparently opposite philosophies of Legalism, as practiced by the statesmen and rulers of Ch'in, and Confucianism—the one despotic, ruthless, and contemptuous of human nature, the other benevolent, stressing moral virtues and behavior—reacted upon each other to create political stability. According to John K. Fairbank, "The Legalist victory, while seeming to destroy Confucianism, in reality created the stable society in which it could triumph. The Confucian victory, far from destroying Legalism, made the Legalist empire all but indestructible."

There were also great advances in art and science. The ignorant might beat drums and bang kettles during an eclipse to drive away the monster that was devouring the sun, but a Han historian had already observed that "Eclipses are regular occurrences. . . . All anomalies and catastrophes are of the same class and are never dependent upon political events." The solar year was already reckoned to be 365 and a fraction days; and the Chinese were already observing sunspots.

Most remarkable of all was the invention of paper. The Chinese were using pure rag paper as early as the second century A.D., more than a thousand years before it was known in Europe. The Chinese themselves say that it was one Ts'ai Lun, an Inspector of Public Works, who first tried making a writing material out of tree bark, hemp, rags, and fishnets, and that he reported the success of this process to the Emperor in 105 A.D. Until then writing had been either on wood or on bamboo strips, the latter often strung together to make a book, which was very heavy; or on silk, which was expensive. The invention of paper gave a great impetus to writing of every kind.

(The use of paper later spread slowly from China to Europe. At the battle of Talas, in central Asia, in 751, the Arabs captured a number of prisoners, including some Chinese papermakers. These were taken to Samarkand, where they taught the art of making paper to the Arabs, and from there it extended gradually through the Arab world, reaching Europe some centuries later by way of Arab Spain.)

The Han Dynasty also saw the beginning of true historical writing. The Chinese had always taken great interest in their history. But now Ssu-ma Ch'ien (about 163–85 B.C.) set a new standard. He kept to the facts as far as possible, recognizing the legendary and supernatural accounts common in earlier histories for what they were; and, when two plausible versions of events differed, he recorded them both, not taking sides.

Ssu-ma Ch'ien's *Historical Record* began with the supposed mythological emperors and came down to his own time, thus including the early years of the Han Dynasty. During the Later Han Dynasty a remarkable family of historians—Pan Piao, his son Pan Ku, and his daughter Pan Chao, the earliest and perhaps still the most famous Chinese woman scholar—followed in his footsteps and produced a detailed history of the entire Han Dynasty. Thereafter China never lacked historians of a high standard, and it became customary for each dynasty to write an official history of the preceding dynasty.

The life of Han times is known to us not only from the histories but from the many delightful tomb figures which have survived. In Shang and Chou times the Chinese had buried bronze vessels in the tombs of their dead; the men of Han, although they did the same, also buried pottery models—models of just about everything that they thought a man might need or enjoy in the next world. There are statues of men and women

Left: A Tower (Tomb figure from the Han Dynasty: 206 B.C.–220 A.D.)—*Courtesy, the Trustees of the British Museum, London*

Below: Men playing a game (Tomb figures from the Han Dynasty: 206 B.C.–220 A.D.)—*Courtesy, the Trustees of the British Museum, London*

—from the rather superior housewife with her hands folded in her sleeves to the charioteer, the night watchman, and the farmer. There is no lack of entertainment: musicians with their instruments; dancing girls swinging their long sleeves; dwarfs; and performing bears. There are models of chariots and oxcarts, and bowmen with arrows drawn; of watchtowers, palaces, farmyards, kitchen stoves, and outhouses. There are superb horses, and laden camels stretching their necks high; dogs, pigs, and other domestic animals.

The pottery vases found in the Han tombs are also of high quality, and they include the earliest known Chinese examples of glazing. Lacquer was widely used, both for decoration and for waterproofing, on all sorts of things: on baskets and bamboo cushions, on wood and on cloth, on shields, sword-sheaths, and other weapons, and even on the spokes of chariot wheels. (True lacquer, which is quite different from the resin lac we use in varnishes, is the juice of the lac tree, native to China. It has remarkable qualities, not unlike those of modern plastics, and is highly resistant to heat and acid as well as being waterproof. The second Ch'in Emperor, Hu Hai, even thought of lacquering the walls of his capital, but had to give up the idea because the surfaces were too large to be properly dried.)

Han architecture is, unfortunately, only known to us from models or descriptions. The palaces seem to have been very similar to those of later years: they were raised on broad stone platforms and approached by flights of marble steps; they had huge round columns to support the sloping roofs; the woodwork of the interiors was brightly painted and gilded, while some columns were apparently inlaid with jade, and some walls were adorned with precious stones.

The Early Han Dynasty came to an end in 8 A.D. when Wang Mang, the nephew of an empress, seized the throne and declared himself the founder of a new dynasty. Wang Mang is often reviled by historians as "The Usurper," as indeed he was; yet, if luck had been with him, he might have succeeded in restoring the great days of Han under another name. Some of his experiments had a lasting influence on Chinese thought, and his attempts to break up large private estates and distribute their land among the peasants have made some writers see him as a socialist born before his time. In fact, he was mainly trying to raise money, being constantly plagued by lack of funds. This was also why he insisted that all Chinese exports must be paid for in gold, not in goods—so successfully that the Roman Emperor Tiberius had to ban the use of silk, which came only from China, rather than lose large quantities of Roman gold.

Wang Mang was less successful in other ways. Nomads raided the north, and the western states conquered by Han Wu Ti reasserted their independence. The river dikes fell into disrepair, the Yellow River changed course, and a series of bad harvests completed the disaster. Neither the poor, who were not noticeably better off, nor the rich landowners who had been deprived of their estates supported the new dynasty. Meanwhile a secret society with strong Taoist leanings, called the Red Eyebrows, organized widespread and successful resistance to Wang Mang.

(Secret religious societies, with such picturesque

names as Red Eyebrows, or Yellow Turbans, were often active in China during troubled times. The most famous, the White Lotus, helped to overthrow the Mongol Dynasty in the fourteenth century, and offshoots of that society persisted into the nineteenth and indeed the early twentieth century, for the "Harmonious Fists" of the Boxer Rebellion in 1900 were directly descended from the White Lotus Society.)

In 23 A.D. rebels broke into Ch'ang-an, murdered Wang Mang, and burned the capital. Two years later a Han prince succeeded in restoring the old dynasty, and established a new capital at Lo-yang. The dynasty thereafter became known as the Later Han, or the Eastern Han.

Under Wang Mang, Chinese influence in central Asia had inevitably receded. But in the first century A.D. the Later Han Dynasty again expanded westward, their task made easier this time because the Hsiung-nu had broken up into several different tribes and were no longer so dangerous. A remarkable general named Pan Ch'ao (brother of the historians Pan Ku and Pan Chao) reconquered the central Asian kingdoms and pushed on as far as the eastern shore of the Caspian Sea. Finally, hearing of a powerful kingdom yet farther west which the Chinese called Ta Ch'in (Great Ch'in) and which is assumed to have been Rome, or at least the Syrian provinces of Rome, he sent one of his men to try and make contact with it.

This traveler had to cross Parthia, and the Parthians advised him that it was impossible to continue his journey overland—although this would, in fact, have brought him quite easily to the oases of Palmyra and Dura-Europos in Syria. When he then turned south, reached the head of the Persian Gulf, and wanted to travel on to Ta Ch'in by sea, the Parthians warned him that the sea was vast, that with unfavorable winds it might take two years to cross, and that many men had lost their lives on the way. When he heard this, he turned back.

The Parthians had good reason for discouraging travelers. They did not wish to lose their extremely profitable position as middlemen in the trade now flowing between east and west across central Asia.

At first this trade had been a matter of occasional embassies exchanging gifts between rulers, but before long the "gifts" were being sold openly and the only purpose of the "embassies" was to transport them. East- and west-bound caravans passed each other on the long, perilous road which stretched for hundreds of miles through barren deserts and over fierce mountain passes.

Silk was China's main export to Rome, and fragments of Han silk have been found all across central Asia and as far west as Palmyra. Furs, iron, cinnamon, and rhubarb were among the other products that traveled from east to west. Meanwhile, coral and pearls from the Red Sea; amber from the Baltic; precious stones, glass, perfumes, and woolen textiles woven in the workshops of Egypt and Syria traveled from west to east. Glass was especially important, for glass was not produced in China itself until the fifth century, and in Han times it ranked with jade and crystal among the most precious materials known.

The insatiable Roman demand for silk, however, meant that the trade resulted in a serious adverse balance for Rome. Gold and silver exchanged for the silk were hoarded in Asia for their own sake, and this drain on Rome's economy was a factor in the economic decline of her empire.

The extraordinary thing was that the Romans knew neither where silk came from nor what it was. At one time they fancied it to be a vegetable matter combed from a certain tree or from animals. As for the source, they knew only that it came from somewhere far east of them; they called this unknown land, and its people, Seres, from the Chinese word *ssu,* or silk.

The Chinese, for their part, had only the vaguest idea of the final destination of their valuable commodity, or even of its final form. Much of the silk exported to Rome was not woven material but silk thread, which was then finished, dyed, and woven into the transparent gauze which Roman ladies preferred (and which led Roman men to protest that their women might as well go naked). When, later, the Chinese first saw these gauzes, they did not recognize them as being made from their own silk.

It was this ignorance on both sides that the Parthians exploited. The Chinese, moreover, seeing how great the demand for silk was, strictly forbade the export of silkworms, or of their eggs, or of any information about the process of raising them. Thus it was centuries before Europeans learned the art of sericulture. Exactly how they discovered it is not clear, but it is thought that some time during the sixth century two Nestorian Christian monks, who were familiar with the process, managed to smuggle out a few eggs of the domestic silkworm in a hollow bamboo tube, and brought these safely to Byzantium. There they explained how the tiny silkworms that hatched from these eggs must be fed on mulberry leaves, how the worms spun cocoons, and how the filaments they spun could be unwound from the cocoons in long, astonishingly strong threads; equally important, how a number of the moths must be bred in captivity each year to produce the silkworms of the following year.

By the end of the sixth century Byzantium was producing enough raw silk to meet its own demands. Other centers were soon established for the raising of silkworms and the manufacture of silk, and knowledge of the industry gradually spread to Greece, Sicily, and Italy. The Chinese monopoly was broken. And no other export from the Middle Kingdom was ever quite so valuable, or had so much influence on the opening up of trade routes from east to west.

7

Centuries of Division (220-589 A.D.)

The Later Han Dynasty, after a gradual breakdown of the administration and the economy of the country, came to an end in 220 A.D. It disintegrated into three separate kingdoms: Wei, based on the Yellow River valley but thrusting westward along the Kansu Corridor and eastward into north Korea; Wu, which occupied the whole of the southeastern bulge of China; and Shu Han in the southwest, roughly modern Szechuan and Yunnan. This is a natural geographic and economic division of the country, and one which tended to recur whenever the central authority weakened. Even in China proper, as we have seen, the north and the south differed in character and were always, to some extent, opposed to one another. The staple crops of the northerners were millet and wheat; their battles were fought from chariots of war; and they had little knowledge of the sea; they were influenced, even against their will, by the people of the northern steppes who were their neighbors. The southerners were dependent upon rice; they were boat-builders, at home on the water, and open to Indian and Southeast Asian influences, which reached them by sea. To these two rivals was added the

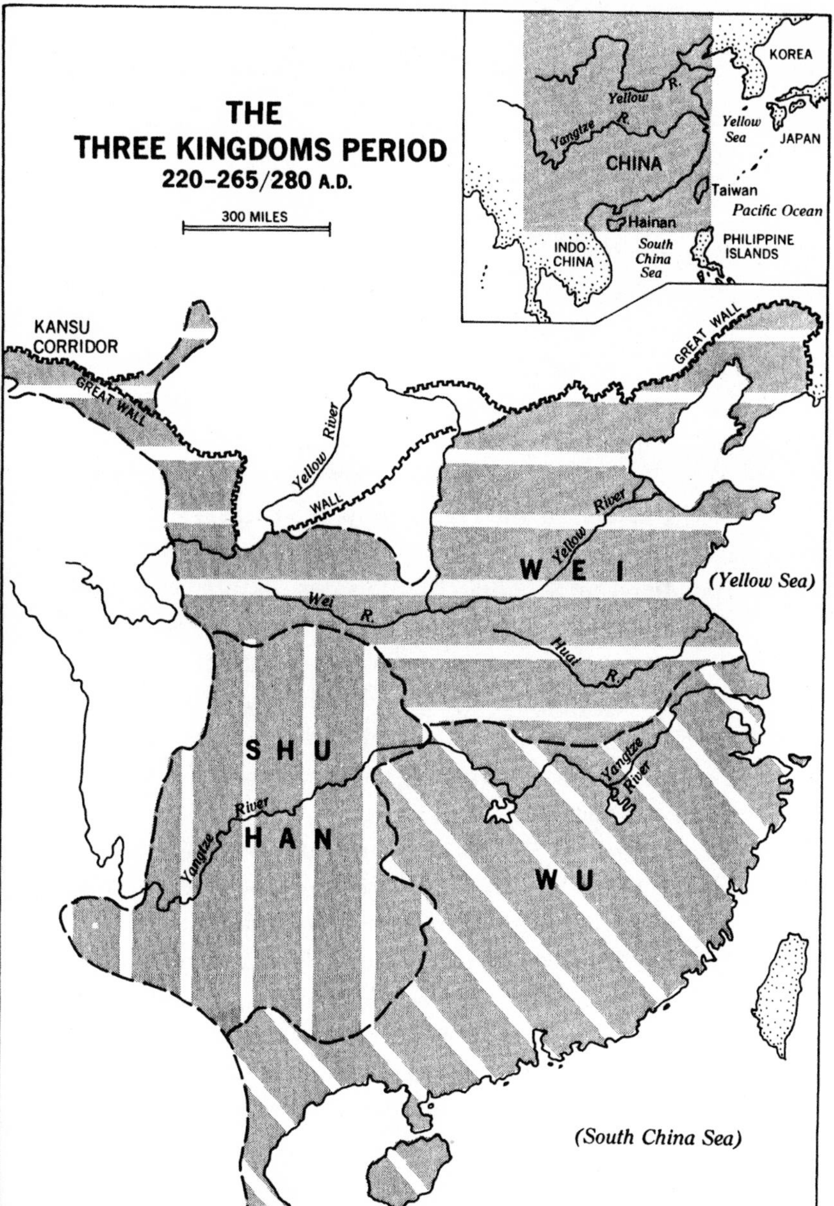
THE
THREE KINGDOMS PERIOD
220–265/280 A.D.
300 MILES
KOREA
Yellow R.
Yangtze R.
CHINA
Yellow Sea
JAPAN
Taiwan
Pacific Ocean
Hainan
INDO CHINA
South China Sea
PHILIPPINE ISLANDS
KANSU CORRIDOR
GREAT WALL
GREAT WALL
Yellow River
WALL
Yellow River
WEI
(Yellow Sea)
Wei R.
Huai R.
SHU
HAN
Yangtze River
Yangtze River
WU
(South China Sea)

southwest: mountainous, difficult land which has always been one of the first areas to break away when China was disunited and one of the last to be brought under control when unity was restored.

The Three Kingdoms period (roughly 220–280), although a time of incessant warfare, widespread poverty, and a sharp fall in population, holds a romantic place in Chinese history. Its heroes are stage figures, larger than life. Ts'ao Ts'ao, a brilliant warrior who overthrew his rivals one by one, reduced the last Han emperor to a puppet, and founded the Kingdom of Wei, is one of the favorite characters in the Chinese theater to this day. Liu Pei, of the Han family, who was Ts'ao Ts'ao's brother-in-arms but later turned against him and founded the Kingdom of Shu Han, is almost equally famous. And one of Liu Pei's generals won such a reputation that he was deified many years later as the God of War, Kuan Ti; temples dedicated to him are found in Korea as well as in China, for the Koreans credit him with driving off a Japanese invasion in the sixteenth century.

Another of the Three Kingdoms' heroes is said to have invented a bow which could shoot several arrows at a time, and some new form of transport described as "wooden oxen and running horses," the nature of which remains mysterious. He is also credited, somewhat dubiously, with the invention of the wheelbarrow.

Whoever first thought of it, the wheelbarrow did, in fact, come into use in China during the Three Kingdoms period, perhaps a thousand years before it was known in Europe. It greatly reduced the manpower needed for small loads, especially on narrow tracks or along mountain roads where there might be only enough room for a single wheel, and was immensely valuable at a time when the country was suffering from underpopulation. Other labor-saving devices brought into general use about this time were the water mill and a primitive machine for sowing seed.

The Kingdom of Wei overthrew Shu Han in 265 and Wu in 280. China was briefly united under the Chin Dynasty (not to be confused with Ch'in), only to fall apart again ten years later. Another three centuries were to elapse before any one ruler was strong enough to reunite the whole of the Middle Kingdom. Meanwhile petty states, kings, and warlords multiplied. Even to list the dynasties that came and went, claiming control over parts of the fallen empire, to name the Liu Sung, the Southern Ch'i, the Liang and the Ch'en, the Northern Wei, Western Wei, and Eastern Wei, among others less important, is to despair of ever sorting them out.

However the pattern changed, north and south remained separate. The whole period is called that of the Six Dynasties, from the number of dynasties which made their capital at Nanking (Nanking, or Nan-ching, means Southern Capital, as Peking, or Pei-ching, means Northern Capital) between the years 222 and 589. The title, however, is misleading, for during much of the time the northern kingdoms were, if anything, more stable and more influential than the southern. As we shall see later, the Northern Wei Dynasty in particular flourished for a hundred and fifty years, an exception to the general chaos and an important landmark in Chinese art.

These centuries are comparable to the break-up of the Roman Empire, a time of political darkness and despair. Yet two things stand out. One is that the Chinese Empire, unlike that of Rome, was reborn to even greater glory without any basic loss of continuity; the T'ang Dynasty was to be the true successor of the Han. The other is that, in spite of the political and economic chaos, warfare, misery, these dark ages saw great developments in art and religion. Beneath the turbulent surface the stream of Chinese culture moved forward. It was also then that Buddhism spread through China.

Buddhism was an Indian religion. The historic Buddha, the Enlightened One, was Sakyamuni, a prince of northern India who lived about 500 B.C. and who was so moved by the suffering he saw around him, by sickness, old age, and death, that he determined to find the cause and cure for the burdens of human existence. Enlightenment came to him one day while sitting in meditation under a Bo-tree. He realized that the cause of suffering is desire, and that only by putting an end to all earthly desires can man achieve the blissful state of Nirvana, or emptiness, which should be his goal. Nirvana is perhaps best described—if one can describe the indescribable—as a state in which the soul is like a drop of water lost in the ocean, yet the entire ocean is contained within the drop.

According to an early tradition, Buddhism came to China because the Han Emperor Ming Ti, on the night of the first full moon of 65 A.D., dreamed that a golden man, more than life-size and shining like the sun, suddenly entered his room.

"My religion will conquer this land," he told the astonished Emperor, and vanished.

When the Emperor consulted his ministers about the

meaning of this vision, one of them suggested that the golden figure must have come from the far west, where it seemed that a new religion had indeed been born. Much impressed, Ming Ti sent messengers off at once across the deserts of central Asia to India, and they returned with two Buddhist priests, a number of sacred writings, and an image of the Buddha painted on cloth. They carried these treasures on the back of a white horse, and the Emperor Ming Ti, overjoyed by the success of their mission, thereupon ordered a Buddhist temple built at the west gate of the capital, and called it White Horse Monastery.

Although rumors of the new religion may well have been widespread by this time, Buddhism itself probably did not reach China until the Later Han Dynasty, a century or more after Han Ming Ti. It became widely accepted there in the chaotic times following the breakup of the Han empire, for it filled a need that neither Confucianism, with its here-and-now philosophy, nor the fanciful flights of Taoism had satisfied.

Buddhism did not supplant Confucianism or Taoism, the second of which also enjoyed increasing popularity at this time. The Buddhists accepted Confucianism as a social code, not a religion; they tolerated the Taoists as men who were less advanced than themselves but were nevertheless seeking the same truth that the Buddha had already found. Thus the three religions of China have existed side by side from the second or third century A.D. until our own time.

With Buddhism, other Indian influences reached China. Not only was literature influenced by translations from Sanskrit; architecture, music, medicine, astronomy, and mathematics all show clear Indian influence from about the third century. The old Silk Road was now become a pilgrims' way, and it is astonishing how many holy men made their way on foot across the whole of central Asia during the next few centuries.

The first famous Chinese pilgrim was Fa Hsien, a Buddhist monk who set out from Ch'ang-an in 399 in search of a complete set of the sacred books of Buddhism in their original language, which did not then exist in China. He made his way across the Takla Makan Desert, which he described as inhabited only by evil spirits and hot winds, where neither bird nor beast could live, and where you could best find your way by following the skeletons of men who had traveled before you. He stopped at Khotan to join in a Buddhist festival there, then went on across the Pamirs —the Roof of the World, as another traveler called those mountains—and down into India. See map on pp. 86-87.

Fa Hsien spent ten years altogether in Buddhist lands, visiting monasteries and holy places, collecting relics and scriptures. He returned to China by sea, a journey almost as perilous as that across Asia, and at the very end of the voyage he was blown off course in a fierce storm and very nearly shipwrecked. He saved his relics and books, however, and on his return to Ch'ang-an he set down *The Record of the Buddhistic Kingdoms,* a full and accurate account of his travels, which was published in 420.

While pilgrims journeyed west, missionaries came east to spread the doctrine, among them one Bodhidharma. So many legends have gathered about this saint that one must view the whole story of his life with skepticism, yet even the legends give some idea of the atmosphere of the time, the piety, the miracles credited to Buddhism, and the readiness with which the new faith was accepted.

Bodhidharma was said, by the Chinese at least, to be the twenty-eighth patriarch, or teacher, in direct line from the Buddha. He left his native India early in the sixth century and traveled first by sea and then overland to the court of Emperor Liang Wu Ti at present-day Nanking. This Wu Ti was the founder of the Liang Dynasty, which ruled south China for half a century (502–555), and was himself an ardent Buddhist, retiring every now and then into a monastery for months of meditation.

The Patriarch seems, however, to have offended his royal host by pointing out that meditation and good works were not enough; a ruler must also possess wisdom and a pure heart. When Liang Wu Ti did not accept his criticisms with sufficient humility, Bodhidharma left the southern court and set out for the north, whereupon the Emperor hurriedly sent messengers to follow him and beg him to return. They reached the shores of the Yangtze just in time to see the saint floating across that great river on a bamboo twig, beyond reach of their shouting.

Bodhidharma traveled on to Lo-yang, then the capital of Northern Wei. There he spent the remaining nine years of his life staring at a blank wall, lost in meditation. This, according to legend, had two surprising results. One was that his legs fell off, since he obviously had no further use for them. The other was that at one point he was so annoyed because his eyelids would keep dropping closed in sleep, in spite of everything he did to keep them open, that he cut them off and threw them out the window. Thereupon he had a vision of the Buddha, who told him that if he would look into the garden he would see his sacrifice had not been in vain.

In the garden, Bodhidharma's eyelids had taken root. Within a short time they grew into a low, fragrant plant, and the Patriarch discovered that the leaves of this plant made a refreshing drink which, moreover, enabled him to stay awake during his meditations. Such was the origin of tea. And this is why Japanese children play with little tumbling figures of Daruma, as the saint is called in Japan, dressed in a red monk's robe, without eyelids and without legs.

Bodhidharma died in Lo-yang. Yet two Buddhist monks who had made the pilgrimage to India about that time and were crossing the Onion Range in the Pamirs on their return journey to China are said to have encountered the saint in the wild mountains there. He was hurrying in the opposite direction, barefooted, carrying one shoe in his hand.

"Where are you going?" they asked.

"To the Western Paradise," he replied, scarcely pausing for breath, and went on his way.

When the monks reached Lo-yang and learned that Bodhidharma was dead, they suggested that his tomb should be opened; in it they found no body, only a single shoe.

Tea was actually known in south China long before Bodhidharma. The earliest reference to it speaks of making a gift "of leaves of tea to take the place of wine" to an official who lived in the third century. Its use spread slowly, however, and probably did not reach some parts of the country until much later, and it was at first valued for its medicinal effect, as a stimulant which warded off sleep. It was not until the eighth or ninth century that it became generally popular as a drink.

The kingdom in which Bodhidharma pursued his final meditations was Northern Wei, founded by the T'o-pa family. It is of great interest as the first comparatively successful combination of a northern, "barbarian" tribe with the rich resources and culture of the Middle Kingdom.

The less civilized northerners reacted in various ways when they conquered north China and found themselves faced with Chinese bureaucracy and an extremely complicated administrative machine, which they were unable to handle. Some simply withdrew, after looting the countryside, and made no attempt to maintain their conquests. Others tried to preserve their own simple way of life by pretending that administration and planning were unnecessary, and that every man could live his own, straightforward life as the nomads did; but this soon led to chaos. Others again employed Chinese to operate the bureaucratic machine, which, of course, meant that the Chinese soon regained complete control of the country, even if they continued to pretend that they were the servants of the conquering race. (It was to avoid this that Kublai Khan in the thirteenth century employed foreigners—Persians, Turks, Indians, as well as Europeans like Marco Polo—in government work.)

The T'o-pas, however, managed to absorb Chinese civilization, to cope with its administrative system, and yet to retain something of their northern hardiness and mobility. For a century and a half they defended

China's culture against other barbarian tribes, encouraged Buddhism, and left behind them in the cave temples of north China a remarkable record of their talents and their faith.

Sculpture had not previously been a major art in China. Early examples of Chinese sculpture are rare, and they are often bas-reliefs—pictures in stone rather than art in the round; the pottery tomb figures are delightful, but not great sculpture. Now, with the inspiration of Buddhism, and with north China ruled by a people who were in touch not only with central Asia but with kingdoms farther west and south, the style of sculpture changed. It was much influenced by what is called the Gandhara school, a remarkable fusion of Indian art and motifs with the form and realism of Greek sculpture. (Greek art had penetrated far into central Asia with the conquests of Alexander the Great, and even when the Greeks withdrew the kingdoms that replaced them carried on the Hellenic tradition.)

Under this influence the human form took on new importance. In the caves and rock temples of Yun-kang and Lung-men, near the earlier and later capitals of the Northern Wei Dynasty respectively, and of Tun-huang, far out along the desert road to India, row upon row of graceful, faintly smiling Buddhas and their attendants are carved from the rock. Some figures are life-size or smaller; some are colossal. Some stand in the round, in deep-cut niches, with pear-shaped, pointed halos; some sit with legs crossed, their hands in the various positions prescribed for different types of meditation or preaching. The bodies are often elongated, slightly twisted, sometimes with a lively sense of movement, but they may also be stolid and stiff, with formal

An apsara, or angel. Stone carving from the caves at Lungmen (Northern Wei Dynasty: 386–535 A.D.)—*Courtesy, Victoria and Albert Museum, London. Crown copyright.*

drapery. It is the faces that still charm the eye—the calm, withdrawn expressions so clearly revealing the faith that inspired their sculptors.

The frescoes and murals of the period, especially at Tun-huang, also have remarkable vitality. Their flying, dancing, lute-playing angels, joyously at home in space, suggest that there were other pleasures in the Buddhist Heaven besides meditation.

Indian, central-Asian, and Greek influences can be traced, and it is likely that some of the artists who chiseled these great statues from the rock were foreigners. Yet any outside influences have been absorbed.

The genius of Northern Wei was to have combined the Indian and Hellenic art of Buddhism with that of China to produce a style of its own. This style not only had a lasting effect on Chinese sculpture; it spread, with the spread of Buddhism, through Korea to Japan, where during the sixth and seventh centuries it inspired the masterpieces of early Japanese art.

8

The Greatness of T'ang

> "By using a bronze mirror you may see to adjust your cap. By using history as a mirror you may learn to foresee the rise and fall of empires."
>
> T'ang T'ai Tsung

TOWARD THE END of the sixth century the ideal of a united China seemed remote. Then, in 581, a northern nobleman—Yang Chien, Prince of Sui—deposed his emperor, took the throne for himself, and some years later succeeded in overthrowing the weak southern dynasty of Ch'en. By the time he died, in 604, the Sui Dynasty which he founded ruled from the Great Wall as far south as Annam, and for the first time since the downfall of the Han the Middle Kingdom, "All under Heaven," was one.

Yang Chien's son Yang Ti (also known as Yang Kuang) is said to have been so impatient for the throne that in 604 he wrote his father's name on a clay model and pierced its heart, with quick results. Like Ch'in Shih Huang Ti, however, Yang Ti is a favorite villain of Chinese historians, always credited with the worst possible motives. If he built warehouses to store surplus grain from the good years to the bad, he was accused of taking food from the mouths of the people. If he added seventeen thousand new volumes to the Imperial Library, he was accused of wanting to fool people into thinking him a man of letters.

The brief Sui Dynasty had, in fact, much in common with the Ch'in, some eight hundred years earlier. Both achieved miracles of unification and construction, but at such a cost, so ruthlessly, that they destroyed themselves, to be followed by the magnificent dynasties of Han and T'ang respectively, which could build on their foundations.

The greatest achievement of the two Sui emperors (there were only two) was to link the major rivers of China with one another by canal. Yang Chien began this work, and Yang Ti completed it, dredging and deepening waterways that already existed, and cutting new ones, until there were, altogether, some four thousand miles of canal. These were not mere ditches; the main canals were forty feet wide, stone-lined, and with willow and elm trees planted so close along their banks that "the shadows of trees overlapped each other" for hundreds of miles.

There were sound economic reasons for linking the north, which was still politically the heart of China, with the Yangtze valley, which was now the more productive area. After the long break between north and south it was vital that communications should be improved, and it was easier to do this by water than by road. Yang Ti, however, also made it an occasion for imperial extravagance. On his inaugural voyage to the Yangtze by the Grand Canal, in 605, he traveled in a dragon-shaped boat two hundred feet long and forty-five feet high, with four decks—one for the throne room and the Emperor's apartments, one for his harem, and two for the servants. The Empress had a similar boat, slightly smaller, and they were escorted by thousands of junks carrying the royal family, the government, and foreign ambassadors. The fleet is said to have been towed by eighty thousand men and to have spread out along sixty or seventy miles of canal at any one time.

Both Yang Ti and his father also raised huge labor gangs to work on the Great Wall. The Wall had fallen into disrepair, for it served no great purpose in the centuries when China was splintered into north and south. The northern kingdoms more often than not had straddled the Wall and included part of the barbarian lands within their rule. Now it was restored, and the weaker sections reinforced, until once again the great rampart stretched from the sea to the desert outposts in the west.

During the Sui Dynasty Chinese traders and pilgrims constantly traveled the Silk Road, bringing back such varied merchandise as lion skins, dancing girls, Buddhist religious tracts, and asbestos. (One may wonder why asbestos was worth transporting across central Asia. It was sometimes used a a candlewick, burning in oil, or woven into fireproof robes, but it seems to have been valued mainly as a curiosity, a "cloth washable in fire," as it is called in China.) Yang Ti appointed a special minister to interview those who had made the journey, and the result was an extremely accurate map and geography of the western regions, with details of their climate, customs, and produce, and of the three possible overland routes thither.

The northern barbarians, although disunited, remained troublesome. Yang Ti tried with some success to play one tribe against another, allying himself with the weaker against the stronger and making a great show of his own power. When he traveled north of the Wall to visit a Turkish khan he is said (although this is doubtless exaggerated) to have had an escort of 500,000 men and a baggage train 300 miles long. When he camped for the night, his servants set up an enormous circle of canvas, on which the streets and palaces of Lo-yang were painted in detail, showing that the Emperor carried his own civilized world with him even there in the barbarous Lands of Grass.

During the Sui Dynasty the population of China increased, which was usually a sign that things were going well. Her frontiers stretched from central Asia to the Gulf of Tonkin. Relations were established with Japan. Yang Ti himself was able, energetic, and ambitious. Yet it soon became clear that he did not have the Mandate of Heaven, and he held the throne for less than fifteen years.

The immediate cause of his downfall was the Korean war. Yang Ti was determined that Korea should enjoy the benefits of Chinese civilization. His advisers tried vainly to persuade him that, if its people were so ungrateful as to resist his efforts, he should leave them to their own unenlightened way of life, and he invaded the peninsula in 612, 613, and again in 614.

The cost of these Korean campaigns, added to his other extravagances, turned the country against him. Rebellion broke out simultaneously on every hand, and the Emperor was forced to flee south beyond the Yangtze River. There he might still have rallied men loyal to him, but he had lost heart, and was perhaps not altogether sane. He shut himself up in one of his many palaces and waited for the end.

"How handsome my head," he is said to have remarked one day, looking into a mirror. "And how graceful my neck! I wonder who will finally sever the one from the other?"

In 618 Yang Ti was strangled by one of his own henchmen. Shortly afterward a man who had been Chief Minister under the Sui Dynasty, Li Yuan by name, founded a new dynasty which he called T'ang. He was succeeded by his son, Li Shih-min, who not only pulled the country together at a moment when its administration might well have broken down, but preserved all that Yang Ti had achieved, so that the history of Sui flows unbroken into that of T'ang and the excesses of the one become the glory of the other.

Chinese emperors are usually called by a dynastic, not a family name, often given to them after their death, and often repeated in more than one dynasty. Thus there was a T'ai Tsung, a Wu Ti, and so forth, in most dynasties, and to be exact one must say *T'ang* T'ai Tsung, *Han* Wu Ti, or *Liang* Wu Ti. T'ang T'ai Tsung (T'ang Great Ancestor) is the dynastic name of Li Shih-min, a name to remember, for he was probably the greatest ruler China ever had.

T'ai Tsung surrounded himself from the first with wise and experienced men. True, other emperors had done the same; the difference was that T'ai Tsung listened to what they had to say and often followed their advice. He liked to sit late into the night discussing history, the strength and the weaknesses of former rulers, and why they had fallen, and he was quick to see how the lessons of the past applied to the future. He appreciated frankness. When it was proposed that a minister whom he trusted should leave the capital on some business or other, he refused, saying that he could not afford to part with a man who he knew would speak the truth to him.

T'ai Tsung liked to point out that Han Wu Ti had waged war for a generation to build an empire, while he, who tried to rule by virtue and example rather than by the sword, had pushed the frontiers of China still farther, into lands so remote that not even grass grew there. He was nevertheless a considerable warrior. Having reorganized the army, increasing the role of the cavalry, he waged a highly successful campaign against the Turks and took their leader's title of Great Khan for himself. He not only brought the Tarim basin (that wilderness stretching from the farthest outposts of the Great Wall as far west as Kashgar, which all central Asian caravans had to pass either on the north or on the south and which was therefore of great strategic importance) under Chinese control, but pushed on westward as far as present-day Afghanistan. Tibet accepted Chinese suzerainty. In the south, Chinese influence and Chinese culture spread still farther into the Indochinese peninsula. Only Korea resisted T'ai Tsung, as it had resisted others before him.

Unlike his Sui predecessors, T'ai Tsung refused to keep up the Great Wall, built and rebuilt with so much agony and loss of life. Walls, he said, created a false sense of security. A nation's strength was in its people and its rulers, not in walls, and with a united people the Middle Kingdom had no need of fortifications.

This may not always have been true, but it was true of seventh-century China. China was then the most powerful and most highly civilized country in the world. While Europe was shadowed in the Dark Ages,

T'ai Tsung's capital at Ch'ang-an was a brilliant, extremely cosmopolitan city, numbering among its people Indians, Persians, Arabs, Tibetans, and Turks from the far west and the north, Japanese and Koreans from the east. Ambassadors are said to have come from Nepal, from India, from Constantinople and beyond, bringing rich gifts. A deposed king of Persia took refuge with his followers at the T'ang court, and many more humble exiles sought sanctuary, bringing their own customs and beliefs.

Religious tolerance seems to have been complete. This was not from any lack of faith or of interest in religious matters. T'ai Tsung argued that truth was to be found under many different names, entered through many different gates; and, like the Great Mogul, Akbar, in the sixteenth century, he liked to hear religious teachers explaining their own faiths even if he did not agree with them. He did not allow his own leaning toward Confucianism, nor the mystical fervor of the Taoists, nor the popularity of Buddhism, to prejudice foreign missions, and refugees fleeing from religious persecution of any kind were welcome in Ch'ang-an.

In 635 Nestorian Christian missionaries reached Ch'ang-an from Syria and were received at the Chinese court. Three years later, after careful study, Christianity was pronounced good and given the Emperor's official approval; this meant that the missionaries were allowed to preach and to establish monasteries. For more than two centuries, until they were driven out during a religious persecution in 845, the Nestorians enjoyed great favor. A commemorative tablet, mounted on a stone tortoise, which described the arrival of the first missionaries and the establishment of the Christian Church in China, was set up in Ch'ang-an in 781 and was still to be seen there as recently as 1966.

Buddhist influence, meanwhile, continued to grow. Another of the famous Chinese pilgrims to cross central Asia, Hsüan Tsang, made the journey during T'ai Tsung's reign and brought back with him hundreds of Buddhist scriptures, statues, and paintings. His travels inspired a delightful book, written in the sixteenth century, and translated into English by Arthur Waley under the title *Monkey,* which describes the supernatural adventures of the pilgrim and his three curious disciples, Monkey, Pigsy, and Sandy.

In T'ai Tsung's day the capital, Ch'ang-an, was a rectangular walled city, approximately five by six miles, with a population of over a million. Its ground plan was very like that of former and also of later capitals, for the Chinese from very early times, influenced by religious considerations, had an ideal plan for capital cities, to which they conformed as closely as possible. The Palace and the Imperial City, where the Emperor and his court lived, were at the north of the city, within their own walls, and were connected with a great Hunting Park immediately outside the city wall. The rest of the city was divided in two by a broad avenue running north-south, with markets and houses on either side and a stream cutting irregularly across the two districts. Many of the larger houses had their own walls, with enclosed gardens and courtyards.

At one side of the city was the Imperial University, which T'ai Tsung enlarged to house three thousand students, many of them supported by scholarships. The

Emperor paid great attention to their studies and to the examinations by which his civil servants and administrators were chosen. These examinations now included Confucian Classics, law, mathematics, history, astronomy, and Taoist philosophy. T'ai Tsung insisted on separating astronomy and astrology and treating the former as an exact science, although under his more credulous successors astrology often took first place again in the study of the stars.

In a book of guidance which T'ai Tsung composed for his heir he advised the boy to model himself, not on his father, who was of moderate virtue, but on the great rulers of the past: "Seeing the highest, you will hold the middle way; but if you see only the middle, you will fall." Despite this modesty, the reign of T'ai Tsung was perhaps the high point of Chinese civilization. Greater artists and poets were to come later, the greatest philosophers had lived before, and there may have been greater material advances under the Han. Yet these early days of T'ang had a freshness, an excitement, and a mellowness which are a rare combination. It came very close to that ideal where the virtue of the ruler ensures the prosperity of his people, and "All under Heaven" moves in harmony.

There is a delightful if unlikely story that T'ang T'ai Tsung was walking outside the Imperial Park one day when he noticed a swarm of locusts in the fields. Locusts were a disaster: when they invaded the country, there was absolutely nothing the farmers could do except watch their crops being destroyed by these apparently insatiable insects.

"Miserable creatures, must you eat the grain?" the

Emperor cried out. "If you are hungry, come feed upon my heart."

His companions tried to stop him, warning him that the locusts might take him at his word, but he replied that he feared nothing for himself so much as to see his people in trouble. Thereupon the locusts rose in a great cloud and flew off, and not another locust was seen that year.

T'ai Tsung died in 649, aged fifty-three, in the twenty-third year of his reign. He was succeeded by his ninth son, Kao Tsung. But already before T'ai Tsung's death the planet Venus had been observed several times in full daylight, a phenomenon interpreted to mean that the imperial throne would be usurped by a woman. The astrologers, at least, were not surprised when, within a few years, a girl of humble birth—who had entered the Inner Courts at the age of twelve—worked and schemed her way to becoming Kao Tsung's empress. First through her husband and her sons, then in her own right, she ruled China for half a century.

Like Empress Lü of the Han Dynasty, Empress Wu is held up as an example of the danger of allowing a woman to hold power. Misfortune, it is said, follows the crowing of a hen. Yet there can be no doubt that she had great qualities. Her beauty, spirit, and ability were admitted even by her enemies, and there was no question of her being a figurehead in whose name wise ministers governed; the major decisions were hers.

Under her authority Chinese armies defeated the Khitan Tartars, threw the Tibetans back from the frontier, and strengthened the garrisons throughout central Asia. Korea, which had successfully resisted

Cast of stone panel from the mausoleum of T'ang T'ai Tsung (Original in the University Museum, Philadelphia)
—*Courtesy, the Trustees of the British Museum, London*

even T'ai Tsung, submitted to her to the extent of becoming a tributary state.

On New Year's Day, 689, she made it clear that she considered herself the supreme ruler by performing religious ceremonies which only the Son of Heaven could legitimately do. She wore the imperial headdress, with tassels of pearl and jade at the front and back (reputedly designed so that, if the sovereign lowered his head, the tassels would shut out the sight of the imperfect world from his superior eyes), and carried the imperial jade scepter. Thereafter she founded a dynasty of her own, introducing changes in ritual and music, and a new flag, and forced all male members of the house of Li (the T'ang princes) to change their name to Wu.

Finally, she claimed to be divine. She discovered a passage in a Buddhist scripture, the Sutra of the Great Cloud, which foretold that the next Buddha-to-be would be born on earth in the body of a woman ruling an empire, and concluded that this must be herself. She had thousands of copies of the Sutra made and built temples of the Great Cloud in every province of China. Then, to prove her power over nature, she ordered flowers to bloom whenever she wished them to —with considerable success, the flowers having been forced in greenhouses. Once, when some peonies she commanded to flower did not obey, she ordered every peony in Ch'ang-an destroyed, and forbade them ever to be grown again.

So firmly did she hold power in her own hands that it was not until she was eighty years old, and ill, that her opponents forced her to abdicate. The T'ang Dynasty was restored.

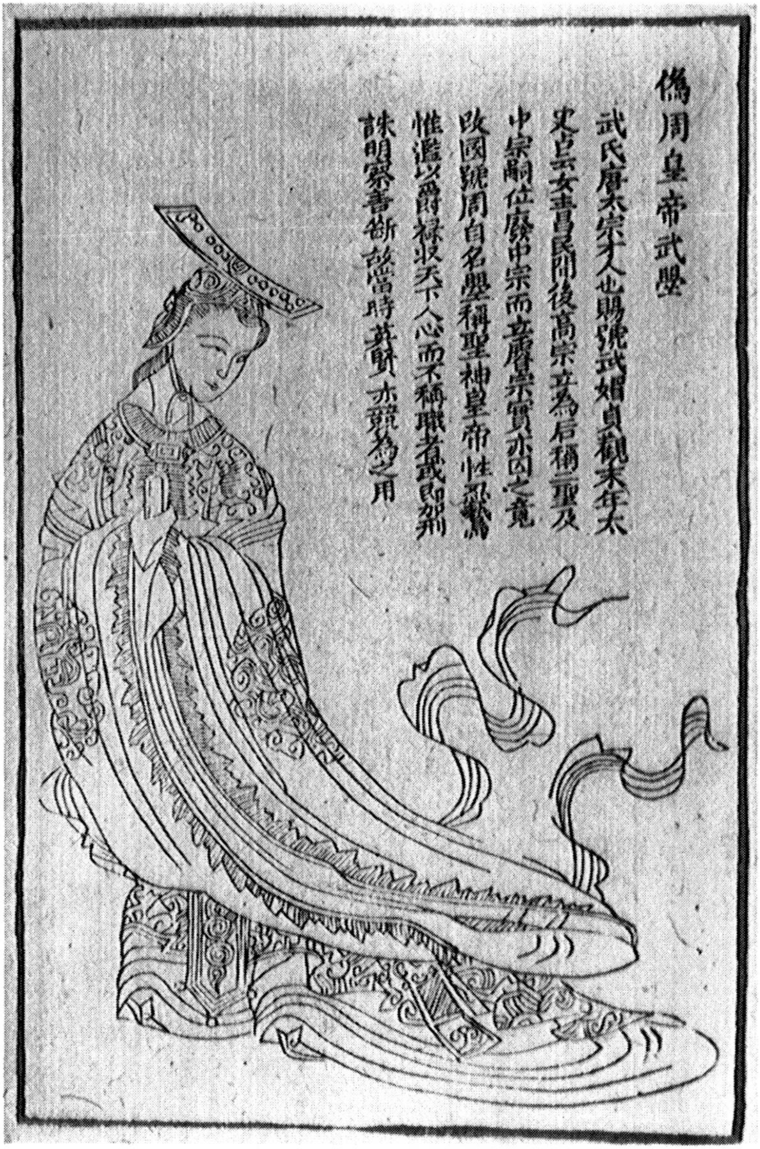

Empress Wu of the T'ang Dynasty: 618–906 A.D. (From a copy of a Chinese book, probably of the 17th century, in the possession of Sir Michael Gillett, K.B.E.)

Had she been Kao Tsung instead of Kao Tsung's wife, the Empress Wu might have been counted among China's great rulers. As it is, the many remarkable achievements of her half century of power are usually credited to the puppet emperors through whom she ruled for much of the time, while she herself is remembered for her cruelty, her vanity, and the excesses of her later years.

9

Twilight of the T'ang Dynasty

THE LONG REIGN of T'ang Hsuan Tsung (712–756), a great-grandson of T'ang T'ai Tsung and better known to us as Ming Huang (from one of his many titles), opened auspiciously. Ming Huang was able, artistic, and intelligent. The Middle Kingdom was peaceful and prosperous. The Chinese Empire extended even west of the Pamir Mountains, while trade not only followed the land route across central Asia, as it had done for centuries, but also moved increasingly by sea. The court at Ch'ang-an was open to foreign ideas and influences, delighting in everything that was new and strange, and seemed at first to have much the same character it had enjoyed under the great T'ai Tsung.

One of the remarkable achievements of Ming Huang's reign was his founding of the Hanlin Yüan, or College of Literature (literally, Forest of Pencils), which remained an important institution down to the beginning of this century. The members of the Hanlin, chosen from those who came out top in the official examinations, were expected to advise an emperor on literary matters, expound the Classics to him in person, and supervise all literary works. They also acted as a sort of College of Heralds, suggesting appropriate reign titles and posthumous titles (i.e., the name by which an emperor was known after his death) for the Son of Heaven, and honorary titles for his various wives. The choice of such names may not seem important to us. But there was magic in a name. An emperor's personal name, for instance, was too sacred ever to be spoken after he came to the throne, and anyone who had the same name must change it. Thereafter the ruler was known by a "reign name," often symbolic of what he hoped to achieve during his reign. (In much the same way the Pope, on taking office, chooses a new name.)

Ming Huang also reformed the system of examinations for public office, which seemed to be in constant need of revision. He strengthened the currency by introducing a monopoly on copper, tin, and lead, which made counterfeiting difficult. A minor but much needed reform was his prohibition against burning clothing or furniture for the dead, as had long been the custom. If it was necessary to provide the dead with worldly goods, he pointed out, paper models of these things should be burnt; it was their spirit which reached the other world, and the spirit of a paper model was just as useful as the spirit of the real thing.

Taking a great interest in astronomy, Ming Huang had columns eight feet high set up at regular intervals from the northern to the southern boundaries of the Middle Kingdom, for use as sundials. Thus the elevation of the sun at different times of the year could be recorded in the different latitudes. He sent an expedition to chart the southern constellations, hitherto unknown in China. Then his astronomers in Ch'ang-an built a detailed model of the heavens, with the earth represented by a box at the center. The machinery that controlled the revolution of the stars and planets around it was concealed in this box, the result being something like a modern planetarium.

An astonishing artistic outburst took place at this time. The eighth century in China was one of those inexplicable periods in history, like the European Renaissance, when the level of talent was so high that it set the standard for centuries to come. An entirely new form of literature also came into existence when storytellers who had formerly recited their tales in public began to write them down for a wider audience. This popular fiction provided a lively, detailed picture of ordinary life, which was missing from the official histories and the Classics.

Among the many great painters Wu Tao-tzu is outstanding. He is believed to have been the first to introduce the flowing brush stroke which was used in writing characters—shading from thick to thin without lifting the brush from the paper—into painting, and he was famous for both landscapes and religious paintings. Once, after he had been on a journey to Szechuan Province to study the mountains there, he is said to have painted "a hundred miles of landscape" on the palace walls in a single day. His work was renowned for realism, and there is a legend that one cave in the last landscape he painted was so realistic that Ming Huang said he felt he could step right into it. "Let us try," replied the painter; and, before the Emperor could stop him, he had bent forward and disappeared into the mouth of the painted cave, never to be seen again.

It was another artist to whom Ming Huang complained that the waterfall he painted on a palace screen was so real that he was disturbed by the splashing of the water. Figures and animals, too, were portrayed with great realism, and some painters spent their lives working on a single subject. When the Emperor suggested to one artist who loved horses that he might study with another whose interests were wider, the painter replied: "Your Majesty, my teachers are all to be found in your stable."

In poetry, too, it was an age of giants. Li Po and Tu Fu were contemporaries of Emperor Ming Huang, while Po Chü-i lived half a century later, and these three were only the most famous in an age when it was said that "whoever was a man was a poet." Li Po is the best known to us. His character comes alive even at this distance, a poet in his life as well as in his verse. He was a wanderer, an idler, a lover of wine, and a Taoist in his approach to nature. Except for a few years when he was at the court of Ming Huang, he remained a poor man. He loved gaiety and the wine-shops, but he also loved remote mountains where he might come across a single fisherman silhouetted in the mist. All this he put into his poetry. His poems are full of color and melancholy beauty; he wrote of spring, of flowers and birds and beautiful maidens, yet behind these there was always a feeling of unworldliness. His friends called him the Banished Immortal, for it was believed that the immortals were sometimes exiled to earth, where they could be recognized by their eccentric behavior and their genius alike.

According to tradition, Li Po was drowned one evening when he was out boating and, having drunk too many cups of wine, mistook the reflection of the full moon in the water for the real moon and leaned over to embrace her. Unfortunately the story is not true; it would have been a fitting end.

Tu Fu was a very different character. Although he too was a wanderer, he was far from carefree. He could not escape from the world as Li Po did, for he was a realist:

> "Before you praise spring's advent, note
> What capers the mad wind may cut:
> To cast the flowers to the waves
> And overturn the fishing boat."

The third poet, Po Chü-i, was born in 772. His best-known work, *The Everlasting Wrong*, telling the story of Ming Huang's love for his beautiful concubine Yang Kuei-fei, was not written until 806. He wrote in simple language, and his verses were popular not only at court but among the people; it was said that one dancing girl put a higher price on her favors because she was able to recite the whole of *The Everlasting Wrong*. Po Chü-i also had a great reputation in Japan, where he was the best-known of all Chinese poets.

The romance of Ming Huang and Yang Kuei-fei is as famous in China as that of Romeo and Juliet in the West. It is perhaps disappointing to learn that Ming Huang was already middle-aged when he first saw Yang Kuei-fei, and that she entered the palace in the harem of his eighteenth son. But it does not destroy the magic that surrounded them. It was the magic of sunset, of a brilliance soon to fade, for Ming Huang's folly not only brought about his own downfall but put an end to the glories of the T'ang Dynasty.

The Emperor was completely captivated by Yang

Kuei-fei, who seems to have been a buxom beauty, with fair skin and a radiant smile. He lost interest in everything except what was of interest to her. And she was constantly seeking new pleasures and new amusements, new favorites and new luxuries, so that the court at Ch'ang-an became a center of gaiety and wild extravagance. The palace was filled with magicians, acrobats, dwarfs, tightrope walkers, and other entertainers. The Chinese theater also came into being at this time, when a group of young actors and dancers (called "Brethren of the Pear Garden," because they held their first rehearsals in an orchard) began presenting operas and plays at the palace.

Performing horses—their bridles heavy with gold and silver and their manes braided with pearls—were trained to dance to music, carrying full wine-cups in their teeth, and to present these to the Emperor and his favorites at the end of the dance. Polo was very popular and was often played in the Inner Courts so that the ladies of the harem could take part, riding horses decorated with bright-colored tassels, bells, and mirrors, and using a wooden ball painted scarlet.

Inevitably, the pleasures of the court were bought at increasing cost. Ming Huang and Yang Kuei-fei might live in a world apart, where the Emperor composed melodies for reed pipe and drum while she danced for his pleasure, content to listen to the poets reciting ever more extravagant verses in praise of Kuei-fei's beauty. Others were more worldly. Yang Kuei-fei's family soon exploited her power over the Emperor. Her three sisters became princesses and built up fortunes of their own, and her brother was made First Minister.

The extravagances of Yang Kuei-fei were not altogether to blame. The great Chinese dynasties seemed to follow a cycle of growth and decay, covering two or three centuries, and the T'ang Dynasty had reached a point in this dynastic cycle when things were likely to go wrong. The aging monarch, too long on the throne, had lost the fire and enthusiasm of his youth. The tax system was breaking down, as it always did when there was no firm control from the central government. Provincial military leaders were openly asserting their independence of the capital. In Ch'ang-an itself there was a struggle for power between the T'ang aristocracy and a new class of bureaucrats who had come into the government through the reformed examination system, which had opened it to a wider range of people from all parts of the country. Chinese authority in central Asia was weakening and now depended on foreign alliances.

This weakness in the Western Regions was not apparent at the beginning of Ming Huang's reign. As late as 747 a brilliant campaign across the Pamirs and the Hindu Kush had prevented a possible alliance between the Arabs and the Tibetans and had seemed to reestablish the Chinese Empire there. This was, however, the beginning of the end. In 751 the Chinese tried to push still farther west and were decisively defeated by the Arabs at a battle near the Talas River. (It was at this battle that the Arabs took prisoner some Chinese who knew how to make paper, and it was thus that paper became known in the West.)

The battle of Talas was a turning point. The tide of the once great T'ang empire had spent itself, and was ebbing. And, although Talas was the last battle fought by the Arabs themselves in central Asia, the forces of Islam which they had led continued to push forward. As Chinese influence waned, the Buddhist settlements strung out along the oases of central Asia were gradually, and permanently, replaced by Islam.

At the other extreme of empire, in the southwest, the Chinese were being pushed back by the Thai. Within the Middle Kingdom itself, meanwhile, one disaster followed another. As so often happened when the political structure was breaking down, Heaven seemed to have turned against the dynasty. The years from 750 to 755 were marked by hurricanes, floods, torrential rains, and other natural calamities; and in 751 a single great fire destroyed two hundred barges fully laden with grain.

In 755 a man named An Lu-shan, the son of a Khitan father and a Turkish mother and thus closely allied to the northern nomads, rebelled against the throne. An Lu-shan had long concealed his ambitions, his shrewdness, and his unscrupulousness under a clown-like exterior, for he was excessively fat, a figure of fun, and no one took him seriously until it was too late. He spent many years at Court, where he became a great favorite of both Ming Huang and Yang Kuei-fei and shared in the revels of the Inner Courts. Yang Kuei-fei was devoted to him, pretended to adopt him as her son, and humored him in every way.

The Emperor placed such trust in An Lu-shan that, when there was trouble in the north, he sent An to take command of the northern army, with headquarters near present-day Peking. This was a strong position, commanding as it did the passes from the north, and it enabled An Lu-shan to build up a following among the frontier tribes to whom he was related. Many of his

Chinese troops were also devoted to him personally; at the frontier their loyalty was to him rather than to the remote Son of Heaven in distant Ch'ang-an.

When, in 755, he raised the standard of revolt and moved south with 120,000 men, his success almost took him by surprise. Within a month he had occupied Loyang, the Eastern Capital, and announced the foundation of a new dynasty.

Ming Huang and his councillors lost their heads completely. Instead of holding the city of Ch'ang-an, letting An Lu-shan overreach himself, and rallying support for the T'ang Dynasty, the Court panicked and fled en masse from the capital, taking with them the soldiers and imperial guards who might have defended the city and leaving it an easy target for An Lu-shan.

The fugitives headed west, taking that mountain road of which Li Po had once written: "It is easier to climb to Heaven than to walk the Szechuan Road." Within two days, however, the soldiers mutinied, murdered Yang Kuei-fei's brother and her sisters and, while protesting their loyalty to the Emperor, demanded that Yang Kuei-fei herself be handed over to them for execution. Ming Huang pleaded with them in vain. Nothing but the death of the favorite would satisfy the soldiers, who by now blamed the whole hated Yang family for the disasters which had befallen the country. Finally, Yang Kuei-fei was strangled by one of the Emperor's own men, and her body was shown to the soldiers, after which the melancholy party of refugees moved on westward.

Ch'ang-an surrendered to An Lu-shan in the summer of 756. On entering the capital the conqueror retired into the Imperial City at the north, surrounded by its own walls, and celebrated the victory with three days of feasting among his comrades and his officers. His soldiers were let loose in the main city, looting, killing, and setting fire to the buildings as they pleased. The beautiful city of the T'angs, the center of the world of its time, was almost completely destroyed.

"In sorrow for the times the very flowers are weeping," wrote Tu Fu. "And the birds flutter in grief at the sad farewell. The smoke of beacons has burnt for three months on end. . . ."

An Lu-shan took a childish delight in being Emperor. One of the first things he did was to order Ming Huang's famous performing horses (those horses trained to dance to music and to carry brimming wine cups in their teeth) to perform for him. But scarcely had the horses started prancing to their usual tune when, one after another, the musicians broke down and wept, throwing their instruments aside, and bowing their heads toward the west, the direction in which Ming Huang had fled. The bewildered animals were soon completely out of control. An Lu-shan, cheated of his new toy, ordered the musicians executed on the spot.

Ming Huang reached Szechuan safely. Meanwhile the Heir Apparent, having had second thoughts, realized that there was still wide support for the T'ang Dynasty both in the army and in the provinces. He turned back, set up headquarters in the northwest, and began to organize what was to be a successful counterrevolution.

Within a year the usurper had been driven out and the T'ang Dynasty restored. Even Ming Huang returned to the capital, an old man, broken-hearted, his only interest in life being to try and communicate with the ghost of his beloved Yang Kuei-fei. He took some comfort when a Taoist priest assured him that she had become immortal and lived on one of the fairy islands in the eastern sea. His dynasty survived for another 150 years. The country regained much of its earlier prosperity, and Ch'ang-an was rebuilt. But the splendor of the great days had gone and would never return.

Toward the end of the ninth century the central authority broke down again, and there were popular uprisings in all parts of the country. These local rebellions were usually put down by the local commanders-in-chief. It was they who now had the power; several among them were so independent that they had, in effect, set up kingdoms of their own. In 907 the most powerful of these rival commanders-in-chief seized the throne for himself, and the T'ang Dynasty was at an end.

The next half century is known as the period of the Five Dynasties and the Ten Kingdoms. The Five Dynasties were those which succeeded one another in rapid succession in the north (so rapid that one statesman held office in four out of the five), while the Ten Kingdoms ruled at different times over different parts of south China.

The situation was complicated by the growing power of the Khitan, a semi-nomadic, Mongol-speaking tribe centered in the valley of the Liao River, who now began to expand into Inner Mongolia and Manchuria. This was the first time that a major barbarian threat had come from the northeast rather than from the northwest of China. The plains and mountains of the northeast, in what is now Manchuria, had until then been sparsely populated by comparatively primi-

Taoist Temple in the Mountains by Tung Yüan—*Collection of the National Palace Museum, Taipei, Taiwan, Republic of China*

tive, disunited nomad tribes and had never exercised the same pressure on the south as the more western tribes.

The collapse of the T'ang Dynasty enabled the Khitan to encroach on China proper. By the middle of the tenth century they had established a kingdom which included parts of north China, with its capital at Peking (which they confusingly called Nanching, or Southern Capital, because they maintained their northern capital in Liaotung). This Khitan Dynasty, which ruled the north for almost two hundred years, was known in China as the Liao Dynasty. But it is from their original name of Khitan that medieval Europe derived "Cathay," and China is still known in Russian as "Khitai."

The political chaos following upon the T'ang Dynasty in the tenth century was similar to that after the breakup of the Han in the third century. The difference was that those earlier dark ages, when north and south had broken apart and dynasties and kingdoms succeeded one another in bewildering number, lasted almost four hundred years. Now it was just over fifty years before the coming of the Sung Dynasty, who, although they never occupied the whole of China proper, were acknowledged to be the rightful successors of the T'ang Dynasty. A united country and a single government had been accepted and taken for granted for so long that, during this half century of civil war, it was regarded as inevitable that it should be restored. It only remained to be seen on whom the Mandate of Heaven would descend.

10

The Sung Dynasty (960-1279)

In 960 the Mandate of Heaven descended, almost literally, upon the shoulders of one Chao K'uang-yin, a leading statesman and general in the last of the short-lived Five Dynasties. The Khitan had recently established their Liao Dynasty in north China, and Chao K'uang-yin was on his way to the frontier to try to prevent their moving farther south. One night, so the story goes, he had retired to his tent and was sleeping soundly when a group of officers who were gathered around the campfire outside and who had been brooding over the state of the Empire, recalling the great days of Han and T'ang, suddenly resolved that they would no longer serve a weak dynasty and an infant Son of Heaven. They threw open the flap of Chao K'uang-yin's tent, roused the sleeping general, and threw a yellow robe round his shoulders, proclaiming him the founder of a new dynasty.

Chao K'uang-yin was a man of ability and noble character, modest in his tastes and generous in his triumph, and during the sixteen years of his reign he brought all central and south China under his control. The Sung Dynasty which he founded lasted for over

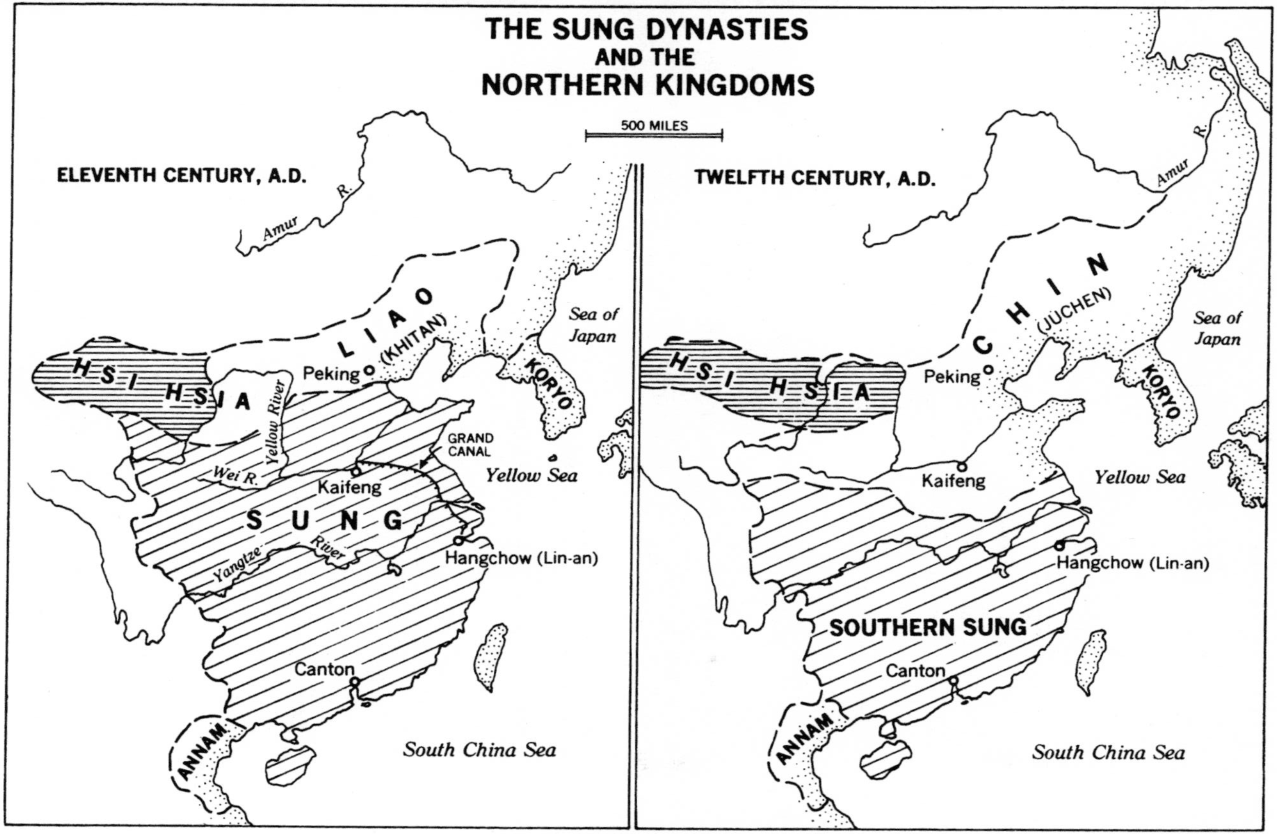
THE SUNG DYNASTIES
AND THE
NORTHERN KINGDOMS
500 MILES
ELEVENTH CENTURY, A.D.
Amur R.
LIAO
(KHITAN)
HSI HSIA
Peking
Yellow River
Sea of Japan
KORYO
GRAND CANAL
Wei R.
Kaifeng
Yellow Sea
SUNG
Yangtze River
Hangchow (Lin-an)
Canton
ANNAM
South China Sea
TWELFTH CENTURY, A.D.
Amur R.
CHIN
(JUCHEN)
Sea of Japan
HSI HSIA
Peking
KORYO
Kaifeng
Yellow Sea
Hangchow (Lin-an)
SOUTHERN SUNG
Canton
ANNAM
South China Sea

three hundred years, until it was swept away at last by the Mongols. The Sung, however, never succeeded in regaining the whole of China, let alone expanding into central Asia as earlier dynasties had done. They were cut off from the north, first by the Khitan and later by the Juchen kingdoms, and from the west by the kingdom of Hsi Hsia, established early in the eleventh century by descendants of the T'o-pa family.

During the early years of the dynasty Sung armies struggled bravely to push back these "barbarians," without success. Later they seem to have resigned themselves to the boundaries of their own extremely prosperous and highly civilized kingdom in the south. The Sung emperors were, on the whole, men of artistic and literary talent rather than of great political ambition or ability. They were also handicapped by not having a cavalry force strong enough to meet the northerners on equal terms; this may have been partly because, without the frontier lands, they were short of pasture for their horses.

The Hsi Hsia, the Khitan, and the Juchen were all much influenced by Chinese culture and could be called barbarian only by contrast with the Middle Kingdom. Their taste for Chinese luxuries was such that when, early in the eleventh century, the Khitan moved south and threatened the Sung capital at present-day Kaifeng, they were persuaded to retire by the promise of an annual tribute of silver and silk. This tribute was increased in later years, and at times the Sung also had to pay tribute to the Hsi Hsia. This constant drain, added to the cost of defense, a steady increase in government expenditure, and a growing population, meant that the Sung Dynasty suffered one financial crisis after another.

The use of paper money became common. Already in T'ang times, so-called "flying money"—something like a bill of exchange—was used between different parts of the country to save transferring large amounts of heavy, bulky copper coins. In 970 a special office was set up to issue what was called "convenient money," and thereafter the circulation of paper money was widespread. Inevitably, there was inflation. Throughout the Sung Dynasty reformers struggled to restore the value of paper money when too much had been printed and people had lost confidence in it. One new issue was even printed on a mixture of paper and silk, perfumed, in the hope of making it more popular.

The most famous Sung reformer was Wang An-shih (1021–1086), an able man, but so inflexible that his enemies nicknamed him the Obstinate Minister. He is described as a socialist, but (like Wang Mang a thousand years before) his socialist measures were meant to improve the country's economy, not to introduce social equality for its own sake. He was a practical man. And he looked at ancient customs with a fresh eye.

For a thousand years and more the percentage of grain paid by farmers to the government in tax had always been sent to the capital. It was transported by canal, in grain barges, which was one reason why every dynasty since the time of Ch'in Shih Huang Ti had spent money and manpower on keeping up the canals and building new ones. The manpower needed was provided by the corvée, a system of forced labor according to which each man, or each family, must contribute a certain number of days' work in the year. Now Wang An-shih proposed to abolish both the corvée and the sending of tax grain to the capital. The grain, he pointed out, could be stored in government warehouses in the larger cities, and sold there, the taxes being sent to the capital in cash.

He also proposed that in certain districts each family should maintain a horse, provided by the government, so that in emergencies a cavalry force could be quickly called up. In education he wanted the students to study practical matters—geography, engineering, medicine, economics, and law—as well as the Classics.

Wang An-shih had great influence with the Emperor, and many of his suggestions were put into practice. But they raised a storm of opposition. Government officials felt that money (often paper money) was not the same thing as grain, and that it would be dangerous to put one's trust in it. There was something solid about those cargoes of grain, moving as they had done for the past millennium, that could never be replaced by any form of currency. As for education, the Classics had been the foundation of all education for so long that the idea of giving equal importance to studies such as medicine and geography was revolutionary. Even before Wang An-shih's death his opponents had won the day, and most of his reforms were reversed.

Wang An-shih claimed to be simply reinterpreting the Confucian Classics. So did almost all the Sung Dynasty reformers, although, in fact, they examined the Classics with a critical eye and used them as they saw fit. They also adapted elements of Taoism and Buddhism to help adjust Confucianism to the world of their time. The result was a school of thought which we call Neo-Confucianism.

The leading Neo-Confucianist was Chu Hsi (1130–1200). He taught that knowledge was the key to understanding, and that men should study everything under heaven. Unfortunately, Chu Hsi's views were so clearly thought out and so well expressed that thereafter most scholars confined themselves to interpreting his interpretation of the Classics rather than looking at the world for themselves. Since his own teaching had been that one should be constantly studying and learning new things, it was ironic that within a few years of his death his philosophy had hardened into a rigid orthodoxy.

This may have been one reason why the traditional philosophy and traditional society of China, dating back to Confucius and the Hundred Schools of Thought, and now set in its "modern" form by Chu Hsi and the Neo-Confucianists, remained almost unchanged for the next six hundred years. Another reason must have been the devastating effect of the Mongol conquest of China in the thirteenth century. The shock of seeing their undoubtedly superior civilization overwhelmed by outsiders, and the Middle Kingdom brought under barbarian rule, forced the Chinese back in on themselves and made them cling to their ancient principles and resist all changes and all foreign influence.

This stagnation of Chinese thought from the thirteenth to the nineteenth century, at a time when Europe was moving rapidly forward, has made us speak of "unchanging China." Europeans have been inclined to view it as both tragic and rather comic. Yet, whatever the cause, six centuries of cultural stability are not to be dismissed lightly.

"In retrospect," as John Fairbank has said, "the Chinese have every right to view with pride the stage in their civilization in which they created a society so perfect within its own guiding ideals and technological limits that it achieved a degree of stability no other high civilization has ever been able to approach."

Although unable to expand territorially, the Sung Dynasty came into contact with the outside world in a new way. Until then, China had looked inland. Her main link with the western world, with Rome and the Middle East, had been the great caravan routes across central Asia. The capital and the heart of the country had been in the north, with a continental outlook. Now, cut off from central Asia by the kingdoms of Khitan and Hsi Hsia, the Sungs moved toward the sea. Their first capital at Kaifeng, although roughly in the same latitude as Ch'ang-an and Lo-yang, was farther east; it was near the junction of the Yellow River and the Grand Canal, the main artery between north and south, and was thus well placed in relation to the seaports of south China. Later, when they were forced to abandon Kaifeng, they made their capital much farther south, below the Yangtze River.

Turning to the sea, the Chinese became boat-builders and navigators. Whether or not the Yellow Emperor had actually used south-pointing chariots in the third millennium B.C., the magnetic compass (still pointing south) was known in China by the third century A.D. and had long been used in divination and fortune-telling. Now Chinese navigators started using the compass to check their course instead of relying on the stars by night.

Their ships probably did not differ much from the high-sterned, extremely seaworthy junks of today. They had sails of matting or cloth, sometimes both, and oars as well, manned by four oarsmen each. They could carry several hundred men, with a profitable cargo, and the wealthier merchants, at least, traveled in considerable comfort. An Arab traveler describes these Chinese junks as having four decks, with separate cabins, and speaks of merchants taking their wives or concubines with them; the crews, he adds, supplemented their diet on the long journey to India and Africa by growing their own plants and herbs in wooden buckets.

These crews must have been extremely skilled not only as navigators but in their knowledge of the coastal waters and prevailing winds, for in the Indian Ocean they made use of the monsoons which blow from the southwest in summer and from the northeast in winter. The ships were built with water-tight compartments, for added safety. They used a balanced, stern-post rudder, and the crew took soundings by means of a deep-sea lead. (Small paddle-wheel boats, manually operated, were also in use at this time, at least on inland waters.) It is not surprising that whereas, in the tenth century, when the Sung Dynasty came to power, shipping in the Indian Ocean and in southeast Asia was almost entirely in the hands of the Arabs, following the great expansion of the Arab empire in the eighth and ninth centuries, by the end of the twelfth century it was almost entirely in Chinese hands.

The trade itself had changed since the days when silk was the major Chinese export. Silk was, of course, still exported, as were lead and tin, but books, paintings, and especially porcelain were in even greater demand. The export of Chinese porcelain to Japan, India, and Indochina at this time was enormous, and fragments of Sung porcelain have been found throughout the Middle East, in Egypt, and along the east coast of Africa.

In the early days of the dynasty, when the sea trade was still largely in the hands of foreigners, mainly Moslems, large foreign communities grew up in the ports of south China, where they prospered and were treated with great toleration. They were allowed to settle disputes among themselves and to administer justice among their own people according to the laws of their own countries. In the twentieth century this privilege, which was called extraterritoriality, came to be considered an insult to Chinese sovereignty because it enabled foreigners to ignore Chinese laws. At that time, however, the Chinese preferred such an arrangement to being held responsible for administering the complicated laws of Islam.

A number of Jews also settled in China at this time, especially at Kaifeng, where they were allowed to build a synagogue and to follow their own religion and their own way of life. The Jewish community there survived until well into the nineteenth century, and Jewish features are still not uncommon in north China.

Gunpowder, like the south-pointing compass, had been known in China for centuries. But, even as the compass had been used only in fortune-telling until a need for it arose in navigation, so gunpowder had been used only in making firecrackers and in some religious ceremonies. Now, however, hard pressed by the Khitan in the north, the Chinese applied the principle of explosives to weapons. By the beginning of the eleventh century they were using primitive hand grenades, or bombs launched by a simple mechanism, and were also experimenting with bullets fired from a long bamboo tube, the prototype of modern firearms. Thus they enjoyed a definite, although brief, advantage over their enemies—brief because it did not take the Khitan long to discover the explosive principle of the weapons and imitate them.

In spite of financial crises, the level of education and the standard of living both rose steadily during the Sung Dynasty. Houses were larger and more comfortable, and the use of ordinary chairs, as well as sedan chairs for traveling, became common. Tea was now the most popular drink, and there were teashops, wineshops, and restaurants in every city.

Printing from woodblocks was by this time common. As we shall see when we come to the Empress Shotoku, of Japan, the invention was a gradual process spread over several centuries. In China, wooden seals were used to stamp an impression in ink on paper—a process very similar to printing from woodblocks—as early as the sixth or seventh century. True block printing probably came into use early in the eighth century. The first printed book still in existence dates from 868, but this is so beautifully printed, and of such advanced technique, that the art of printing must have been known many years earlier. By the time of the Sung Dynasty books of every kind—prose, poetry, history, encyclopedias, and textbooks—were being printed. In fact it would seem that all the important Chinese literature then in existence was printed during the Sung Dynasty. This ease of production led, in turn, to an increased literary output.

Another popular use for printing was in playing cards, or sheet-dice, as they were first called. The Chinese, who are great gamblers, were using printed playing cards at least as early as the Sung Dynasty.

The abacus, or counting board, also came into use toward the end of the dynasty, and is still in use today. It consists of a shallow case, divided into two unequal sections by a crossbar, with wires or bamboo rods running at right angles to the bar. Beads of bone or ivory, five on one side and two on the other, having different values, make it possible to do complicated sums with astonishing speed, and the click of the beads on an abacus is a familiar sound in many Far Eastern shops.

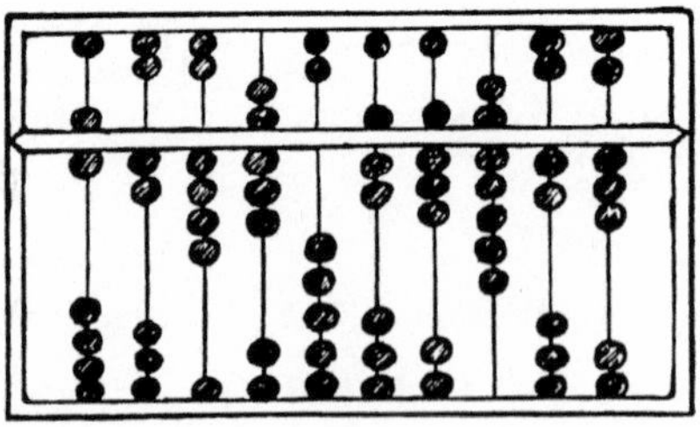

Abacus

At this time the Chinese began to take great interest in their past—not just in their history or their literature, but in everything that had come down to them from past ages. Scholars collected ancient bronzes, books, inscriptions on stone, paintings, and even temple bells, and wrote about these things in great detail.

Modern historians have taken much of their material from the Sung scholars.

Sung porcelain was perhaps the finest ever made anywhere in the world, both in form and in the glazes and techniques used. It was deliberately austere in line and color, often pure white or the delicate gray-green shade known as celadon. (Celadon, surprisingly, takes its western name from a character in a French play of the seventeenth century, who wore a costume of that color.)

Sung painting was also superb. Chinese writers generally assume that the T'ang Dynasty was the high point of Chinese painting, which may well be so; on the other hand, little if any original T'ang painting remains to us, and it is possible that, whereas the great T'ang painters introduced new ideas and a new technique of flowing brush strokes, Sung artists brought these to perfection. Their landscape ("mountain-water") painting shows those misty hills and winding lakes, those jagged rocks and shadowy pine trees, which seem to us in the West to express the essence of Chinese art. The new Chinese interest in the sea appears in seascapes, which were the specialty of at least one Sung painter.

In sculpture the Sung Dynasty was inferior to the T'ang. With the decline of Buddhism there was less inspiration, less need to reproduce the human form in statues or in bas-reliefs. Tomb sculpture was also much less important than in Han and T'ang times, possibly because people were more sophisticated.

One custom that came into being during the Sung Dynasty was to cause untold misery through the cen-

"Conversation under the Pine-cliff." Painting by Hsia Kuei (Sung Dynasty: 960–1279)—*Collection of the National Palace Museum, Taipei, Taiwan, Republic of China*

turies: the custom of binding women's feet. Why, no one knows. Small feet were always considered attractive, and the habit of binding them tightly to make them smaller may have originated among the ballet dancers of the time. Once the custom was established, both the tiny, deformed feet and the curious walk that they induced were apparently so attractive to the opposite sex that women were afraid their daughters would never find a husband unless they had it done. The actual process involved binding the feet of girl children from the age of five or six more and more tightly, in such a way that, as the foot grew, the arch was broken and the toes bent under, the foot being finally so deformed that it was only three or four inches long. The custom persisted from Sung times until the twentieth century, among all classes of women.

Early in the twelfth century a Tungusic people known as the Juchen rose to power in the northeast. By 1125 they had driven out the Liao Dynasty founded by the Khitan two centuries before, and had established their own. They called this the Chin, or Golden, Dynasty, and they too made their capital at Peking. The Sungs, meanwhile, underestimating the strength of these new barbarians, had rashly formed an alliance with them against their old enemies, the Khitan. Once the Khitan had been eliminated, however, the Juchen broke the alliance, swept down on the south, occupied the Sung capital at Kaifeng, and captured the Sung Emperor Hui Tsung. (It was typical of Sung emperors that Hui Tsung was a first-class painter but not a strong ruler.)

This looked like the end of the Sungs. Yet they rallied their forces, held central and south China, and established a new capital south of the Yangtze River at Lin-an (modern Hangchow). Thereafter the dynasty is known as the Southern Sung; and, until they were overwhelmed by the Mongols, 150 years later, their kingdom was among the richest, most luxurious, and most highly civilized ever known in China—or in the world.

In the late thirteenth century Marco Polo, who came from Venice and had seen many of the other great cities of his time, visited Lin-an, which had only recently been captured by the Mongols (and which he called Kinsai). Even then, under alien rule, he described it as the Celestial City because of its "pre-eminence to all others in the world, in point of grandeur and beauty, as well as from its abundant delights, which might lead an inhabitant to imagine himself in paradise."

11

The Mongol Empire

> "Therefore, son of man, prophesy and say unto Gog, Thus saith the Lord God . . . thou shalt come from thy place out of the north parts, thou, and many people with thee, all of them riding upon horses, a great company, and a mighty army . . . and the mountains shall be thrown down, and the steep places shall fall, and every wall shall fall to the ground."
>
> Ezekiel, 38

THE SUDDEN RISE of the Mongols at the beginning of the thirteenth century, and their drive westward to the Black Sea, the Persian Gulf, and Europe, were almost incredible. Many Europeans at the time believed them to be the people of Gog and Magog described by Ezekiel. Even centuries later one can feel the terror inspired by those wild horsemen, and marvel at the distances they covered.

It is true that no single great power opposed them. Even Khorezm, the largest of the Turco-Persian Islamic states which had replaced the Arab empire in western Asia, although outwardly powerful, was in decline. Europe was divided. The kingdoms of Hsi Hsia and Juchen had reached the end of the cycle of growth and decay that seemed to govern such empires; so had the Southern Sung. The nomad economy, moreover, could be shifted from peace to war overnight in a way that was impossible for settled communities. Yet, when all this has been said, the Mongol victories remain fantastic. At the end of the twelfth century the man who was to become Genghiz (or Chingis or Jenghiz) Khan was the leader of a small nomad tribe in northern Mongolia; when he died in 1227, he had eliminated the Hsi Hsia, driven the Juchen south of the Yellow River, and started his armies on the course that was to overrun Mesopotamia, Persia, and Russia, as far west as Moscow, as well as Korea, China, and much of southeast Asia.

Temujin, the future Genghiz Khan, was born about 1167. His father, chief of a Mongol clan, died when he was still a boy, and he had to fight for his inheritance. His military genius was soon obvious. The inter-tribal warfare, between comparatively small numbers of comparatively well-matched nomads, in which he first engaged, may seem a simple matter compared with campaigns carried on against established kingdoms a thousand miles away. On the contrary; success in these tribal wars required quite exceptional qualities of leadership. A man who could both conquer and hold the allegiance of the nomad clans was well qualified for the conquest of more civilized nations.

Clan by clan and tribe by tribe, Temujin either defeated or won over his rivals, until the people of the desert and the steppe were united as never before. It was a slow process; but in the Year of the Leopard, 1206, "all the generations living in felt tents became united under a single authority," and the tribes assembled in conclave to acclaim Temujin their ruler, with the title Genghiz Khan.

This uniting of the tribes into a single Mongol nation released the energies that had formerly been dissipated in tribal warfare, and the Mongol armies exploded outward, spreading destruction across the medieval world. North China was overrun, and the heavily fortified Chin capital was destroyed in 1215, although remnants of the Dynasty held out for some years south of the Yellow River. By 1220, Mongol forces had captured Samarkand and Bokhara, and within the next two years they had crossed the Oxus and had conquered the kingdom of Khorezm. They reached the banks of the Indus in 1221, and only turned back from India because the alien climate caused sickness among them. The kingdom of Hsi Hsia was eliminated in 1227.

The size of the Mongol armies was vastly exaggerated by their contemporaries. Their victories were won by organization, discipline, and brilliant strategy. The numbers engaged were relatively small. Genghiz mobilized 150,000 soldiers for the war against Khorezm, where they were opposed by 400,000. The forces he led against the Chin were less than a quarter of theirs.

The Mongol striking force consisted entirely of cavalry, with several horses to each rider, and was thus extremely mobile. Their horses were small, hardy creatures that could outlast any Arab thoroughbred; they needed little water and were capable of traveling great distances over rough country under a full load and with very little rest. And the Mongols themselves were always more at home in the saddle than on foot. They learned to ride from the age of three, sometimes tied to the saddle, and by four or five were allowed to shoot from horseback with bow and arrow. Archery was literally child's play to a Mongol. Their wooden saddles, rubbed with fat to keep them from cracking or swelling, were built high both front and back so that the rider was held steady when shooting.

The Mongols used both light and heavy bows. Their heavy bow needed a stronger pull than that of the famous longbow of the English yeoman, and its range was between two and three hundred yards. They also carried a lance, with a hook for pulling their enemies from the saddle, a saber, and sometimes a mace. Their armor, which was also fitted to the horses in the front ranks, was made either of thin iron scales, overlapping, or of layers of hide, softened by boiling, sewn tightly together, and lacquered to keep out the damp. They also carried shields, although these were mostly used when fighting on foot or besieging walled cities. In the field every man traveled with a sheepskin coat and a fur helmet, a lasso, a hatchet, a cooking pot, a file for sharpening arrow heads, two leather bottles for water, and a leather bag to keep his equipment dry when fording rivers.

Soldiers were trained to sleep in the saddle, letting their horses graze through the night. On long campaigns they carried a ten days' ration of food which needed no cooking; dried meat, dried milk curd, and koumiss, or fermented mares' milk. If necessary, according to Marco Polo, they would open a vein in their horse's neck and drink the blood.

The Mongols also employed more sophisticated weapons such as espionage and psychological warfare. Before every campaign Genghiz sent scouts to bring back detailed information about rivers, roads, mountain passes, and fortified cities. He used the Moslem merchants who were constantly traveling back and forth across the trade routes of central Asia to discover the economic and military strength of kingdoms he planned to attack. It was thus he learned that the apparently powerful kingdom of Khorezm was in difficulties, whereupon he struck at once.

Being so well informed, Genghiz could take advantage of any dissension among his enemies, and on occasion he forged letters to turn one against another. He encouraged rumors that the Mongol hordes were larger than they were, and in battle he created the same impression by tying branches to his horses' tails, so that they stirred up the dust behind them, as though a huge army were following; he lit campfires where there were no camps, and mounted dummies on spare horses.

His strongest weapon was fear. Terror spread before the advancing Mongols, not without reason, for they massacred, looted, and destroyed whatever stood in their path as pitilessly as a swarm of locusts. The entire population of a city might be put to the sword. Or the women and children might be taken as slaves, the city razed, and the men forced to lead the assault on the next city to be besieged; this was almost the same as massacring them, and saved Mongol lives. This terrorism, this absolute ruthlessness, may have been exaggerated. A city was sometimes spared if it surrendered at once. There was no religious persecution as such. And we must remember that the Mongols were not alone in their time; other armies in Asia and in Europe massacred their enemies without pity during the twelfth and thirteenth centuries. The atrocities of the Mongols were only on a greater scale, more efficient, perhaps more irrational. When Genghiz conquered the Hsi Hsia, his men were disappointed to find the land cultivated, with scant pasture for their horses, and urged their leader to wipe out the entire population so that they could convert the land to pasture. It was only when Yeh-lü Ch'u-ts'ai (an adviser of whom we shall hear more later) pointed out that as a subject race the Hsi Hsia could provide the Mongols with bows and arrows, grain, wine, and other tribute, whereas, if they were exterminated, the country would yield only grass, that the Khan agreed to spare them.

Invincible in open country, the Mongols were sometimes stopped by walls. Although they swarmed across the plains of north China in 1211, they were unable to capture the strongholds of the Great Wall. When they launched a second attack in 1213, they found the main fortress still impregnable. The ground was thickly strewn with caltrops (a caltrop is a four-spiked iron ball that will maim any horse treading upon it), and the north gate of the fortress had been sealed shut with molten iron, so that even if the defenders wanted to surrender, they could not open it. Finally, unable to force the gate, Genghiz had to outflank it, breaking through another gate in the Wall to the southwest and storming the main fortress from the rear.

The advancing Mongols were halted again at the Chin capital. The Chin rulers had built truly mammoth city walls, with a triple line of moats and four separate fortresses on the four sides of the city, connected with the capital by underground tunnels. It was impossible

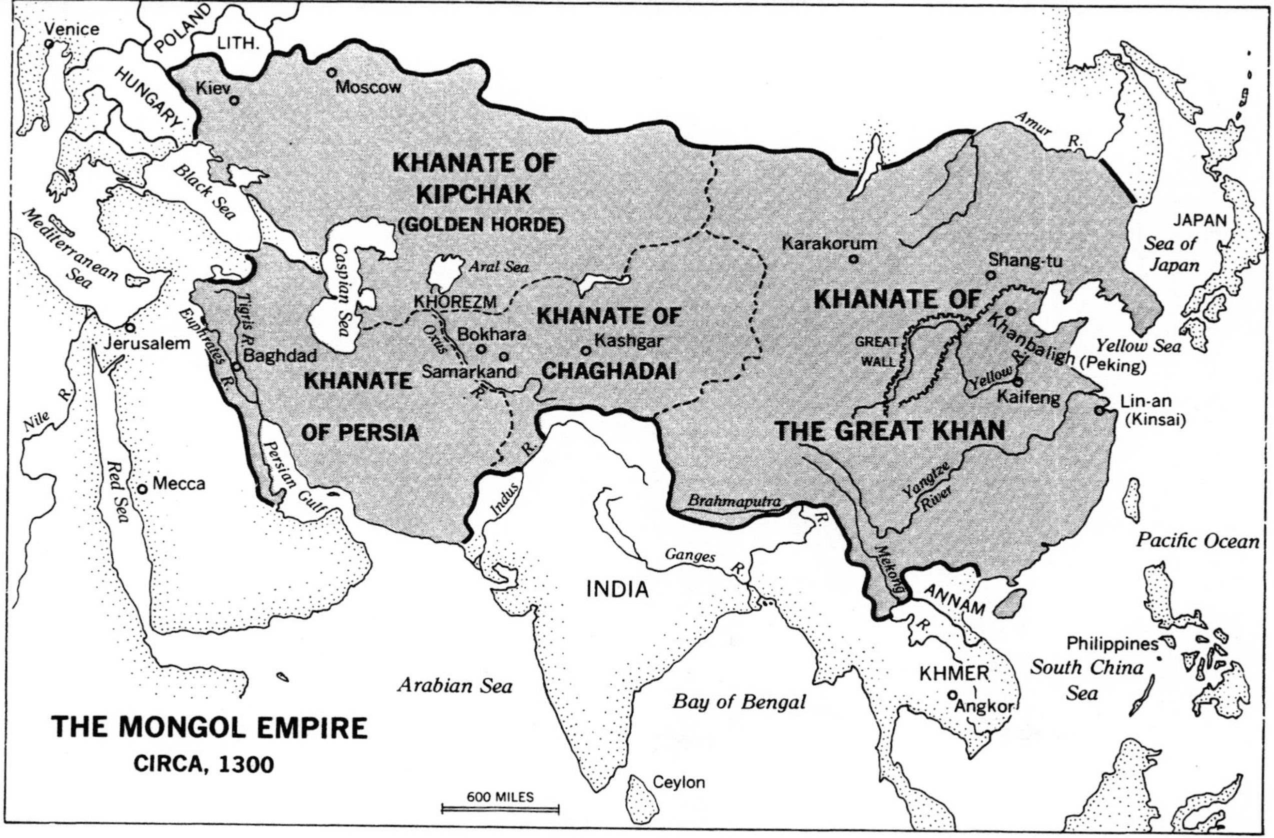

THE MONGOL EMPIRE
CIRCA, 1300

to approach the city from any direction without meeting crossfire from these forts, and the Mongols had to retire.

The Chin Emperor, however, could read the writing on the wall. He abandoned the capital to its fate, moving his court south to Kaifeng. Genghiz Khan took the city at last, in 1215, and burned it to the ground. Months later the ruins still smoldered, and the bones of the dead were heaped in great mounds outside the broken walls.

In the general massacre the Great Khan spared men who might be useful to him: mathematicians, astronomers, skilled workmen, administrators, men he needed in his growing empire. Among the survivors of Peking was Yeh-lü Ch'u-ts'ai, a descendant of the royal house of Khitan (the Liao Dynasty, which had preceded the Chin). Genghiz pointed out to him that as a Khitan he must be grateful for the downfall of the Chin.

"I have served the Chin Dynasty all my life, as my father before me," said Yeh-lü Ch'u-ts'ai. "I cannot rejoice in their sorrow."

Genghiz Khan was much impressed by this answer. Yeh-lü Ch'u-ts'ai became one of his most trusted ministers, and undoubtedly helped to establish the Mongol empire on a firmer basis than would otherwise have been possible. Under both Genghiz and his son Ogodai, he showed the Mongols how to make the most of their conquests, and how to use the talents of the Chinese and other foreigners to provide skills which the Mongols themselves lacked. His counsels of mercy must have saved thousands of lives.

Genghiz died in 1227, at the end of the campaign against the Hsi Hsia. His body was taken north for burial; and, according to Marco Polo (although his account may have been based on a misunderstanding), whenever the funeral procession met anyone upon the way the soldiers immediately put him to death, crying out: "Go, serve your lord in the next world!"

The Mongols, however, have never believed that he is dead. Like other great national heroes—such as King Arthur, or the Emperor Frederick Barbarossa, who lies spellbound in a cave in Germany—Genghiz is believed to be sleeping the centuries away. One day, the Mongols say, he will return. Meanwhile his spirit undoubtedly lives on. Even the Chinese Communist government has tried to win Mongol support by building a mausoleum for the supposed relics of Genghiz Khan.

Genghiz was succeeded as Great Khan by his son Ogodai. Under his leadership the Mongol armies swept on to further conquests, overrunning the remaining pockets of independence or rebellion until the whole vast empire was one. His successors were able to turn their attention to the administration of the conquered territories.

Savage in war, the Mongols in peace were extraordinarily tolerant. By making use of talent where they found it, they created an empire the like of which had not been seen before, and has not been seen since. In the century—roughly from the middle of the thirteenth to the middle of the fourteenth century—when the Mongol writ ran from Europe to southeast Asia, they succeeded in uniting the greater part of the civilized world under one ruler and one code of law. The roads from Europe to China, closed for centuries, lay open to all—to traders, missionaries, scientists, ambassadors, and fortune-hunters. Already, in 1219, Genghiz Khan had started building new roads for the use of his invading armies, and these continued to be extended and improved in peacetime. The Mongols, moreover, maintained stations, twenty-five or thirty miles apart, across the whole of central Asia, providing food and shelter for any traveler who had the Khan's approval as well as for the official couriers. The latter, using relays of horses, and binding their heads, chests, and bellies tightly in order to lessen the strain on their bodies, could cover two hundred miles a day, a record for pony express probably never equaled elsewhere.

The Mongols' westward drive came to an abrupt end in 1241. Western Europe was saved from an invasion that seemed imminent and likely to succeed. The reasons for this sudden withdrawal of an apparently invincible army are not altogether clear. It may have been because the death of the Great Khan Ogodai meant that there had to be a gathering of the clans to choose his successor. For some years after Ogodai's death, moreover, the Mongol leadership was weak or divided; it was only with the accession of Mangu Khan in 1251, and of his brother Kublai in 1260, that the Mongol empire again came under a strong ruler. Yet Mongol armies had been withdrawn overnight on other occasions, causing a contemporary to exclaim, "God knows whence they came, or whither they have gone!"

An extraordinary change in the European attitude to the Mongols took place within the next few years. As early as 1245 the Pope sent an ambassador, Friar John of Plano Carpini, to the Mongol court at Karakorum to beg help against the Saracens; in 1253 King Louis IX of France sent Friar William of Rubruck on a similiar mission. This, we must remember, was still in the time of the crusades, when Islam was the principal enemy of Christendom. Thus, no sooner was the threat of Mongol invasion lifted than Christian rulers began to look to the East for possible allies against the Moslems.

One reason for their surprising optimism was the belief that a Christian monarch, one Prester John, was all-powerful in central Asia. This legendary Prester John can be identified with Ung Khan, the (Nestorian) Christian king of a tribe to whom Genghiz Khan swore allegiance in his youth, and whom he later overthrew. But the legend goes deeper than that. Already in 1165 the Pope, Frederick Barbarossa, and other Christian rulers had received a letter from "Prester John," describing the marvels of his kingdom, and how, when he went forth to war, he was preceded by thirteen huge crosses made of gold and jewels, carried in thirteen chariots, to show his devotion to the faith. He intended, he said, to visit Jerusalem and to "chastise the enemies of the Cross of Christ." He had, it seemed, already set out for Jerusalem once before but had turned back after waiting in vain for the Tigris River to freeze over during the winter, as rivers in his country did.

The letter was, of course, a forgery, for reasons unknown, but it had an extraordinary effect. Belief in the existence of this fabulous Eastern potentate remained unshaken by the fact that no one was able to locate his supposed kingdom. Only gradually, as more and more travelers visited China and central Asia, did it become clear that, although there were a number of Christians and Christian churches in the Mongol empire, Prester John was a myth. During the fourteenth century he quietly disappeared from Asia and reappeared in Abyssinia, where the legend of a mysterious

Portrait of Kublai Khan (artist unknown)—*Collection of the National Palace Museum, Taipei, Taiwan, Republic of China*

but all-powerful Christian monarch lingered on until modern times.

The Mongol conquest of south China was slow by comparison with their other campaigns. The country south of the Yangtze was unsuitable for cavalry, and the Southern Sung were strong on their own ground. They had walled cities, heavily fortified; gunpowder and explosive weapons; huge catapults operated by a hundred men; and a strong naval force both at sea and on the inland waterways. It was not until 1279 that Kublai Khan could claim the whole of the Middle Kingdom as his.

The Sung navy captured by Kublai enabled him to extend his conquests overseas. The genius of the Mongols, however, was in land warfare; they remained horsemen at heart, and the sea was alien to them. Their two attempted invasions of Japan failed. They did much better in southeast Asia, where their expeditions ranged far and wide. In Vietnam their armies more than once occupied Hanoi, while in Burma they advanced to the valley of the Irrawaddy River and occupied Pagan. Appearing with a Chinese fleet even as far away as Java, they intervened in the affairs of that kingdom, helping a new ruler to establish himself on the throne. But, although these and other, smaller countries acknowledged the suzerainty of the khans for a time at least, and sent tribute, the Mongol conquests here were short-lived.

They did, however, have some lasting effects. For one thing, they spread abroad greater knowledge of China and its culture and thereby reduced India's influence in southeast Asia, which had been very strong.

For another, the Mongol incursions left behind, in at least one country, deep and bitter memories: in Vietnam the Mongol invaders of the thirteenth century have continued to be an object of execration down to this very day, and the name of the Vietnamese leader who finally defeated them occupies a hallowed place in the pantheon of Vietnam's national heroes.

The Mongol adventures in southeast Asia also resulted in the only detailed contemporary account we have of Angkor, the magnificent capital of the Khmer Dynasty, in modern Cambodia, which was written by a member of a Chinese embassy sent there in 1295, in the time of the Mongols.

Kublai Khan took the name of Yüan for the dynasty he established in China. He kept the administrative structure of T'ang and Sung (this, in fact, with its Six Ministries, remained basically unchanged from the seventh to the twentieth century), but he tried to keep it from being dominated by the Chinese scholar-gentry, employing as many foreigners as possible, Turks, Persians, and Europeans among them. The Mongols had already adopted the Uighur Turkish script for their written language, which made them less dependent on Chinese bureaucracy. The Uighur script, having come by various stages from the ancient Phoenician, was alphabetic, and therefore more easily adapted to another language than Chinese characters.

Kublai Khan moved his capital from Karakorum, in outer Mongolia, to Khanbaligh (City of the Khan, the Cambaluc of Marco Polo). This was on the site of modern Peking, where the foundations of its walls are still to be seen, and from Marco Polo's detailed description of its magnificent palaces they must have been very like those of the present Forbidden City there; single-storied halls raised on broad marble platforms, with steeply sloping roofs; the interiors ablaze with gold, silver, and bright colors. But what most astonished foreign travelers was the artificial hills and lakes, the great hunting parks, the animals who came to drink at streams diverted through the city, all of which the Great Khan had introduced to remind him of his native wilderness.

Wu-men: Gate in the Forbidden City, Peking—*Photograph by Gillian Wilson*

Even so, Kublai Khan spent only the winter months at Khanbaligh. He built a summer capital about fifty miles north of the Great Wall, ten days' journey from Peking, and called it Shang-tu, or Upper Capital. This was the city which inspired Coleridge's poem:

"In Xanadu did Kubla Khan
  A stately pleasure-dome decree;
Where Alph, the sacred river, ran
  Through caverns measureless to man
Down to a sunless sea."

In this Mongol century, when Europe and Asia lay open to each other, many Western travelers visited China. Most famous among them is Marco Polo, the Venetian. He was a lad of seventeen when, in the year 1271, he set out with his father and his uncle (who had already visited the court of Kublai Khan and returned) on a journey which was to last for over twenty years. Travelers in those days thought little of spending a winter or even a year at different places along the way, and it was not until the summer of 1275 that the three Venetians reached the court of Kublai at Shang-tu. They were well received, and the Great Khan took a particular liking to young Marco, who must have been an intelligent, observant lad, quick to learn the language and the customs of the Mongols.

The Polos stayed in China for seventeen years, employed in government service, and Marco made several trips into the interior and as far south as Burma. In 1292 the Great Khan somewhat reluctantly agreed that the three Venetians, who were skilled navigators, should accompany a Mongol princess whom he was sending to Persia as a wife for the Persian khan. Thus the Polos left China by sea, reaching Persia two years later after a journey so hazardous that several hundred men are said to have lost their lives. From Persia, in 1295, they traveled on to Venice, where they heard the news that their patron, the Great Khan Kublai, had died.

Venice was then at war with Genoa. Marco Polo

took command of a Venetian galley, was captured, and spent three years as a prisoner in Genoa. It was there that he dictated his famous *Description of the World* to a fellow prisoner. This was dismissed by his contemporaries as a wild traveler's tale, and it was only long after his death that people realized what an accurate observer he had been—that, when he spoke of black stones being dug out of mountains and used as fuel, he meant coal; that, when he spoke of a mineral which could be split into fibers, woven into cloth, and then thrown into the fire to be bleached, he meant asbestos; that, when he described the splendors of the Great Khan's court, the speed of his couriers, the use of paper money in exchange for goods, the beauty of the ancient capital of Southern Sung, he was stating facts.

In spite of the many travelers between East and West, the Yüan Dynasty was not a period of artistic originality. Western influence was mainly in details; it did not spark off an artistic renaissance.

Popular writing, however, came into its own at this time, and the novels and plays of the Yüan Dynasty are among the most famous in Chinese literature. This may have been partly because of the literary leanings of the Mongols themselves; partly because fiction allowed Chinese writers, restless under alien rule, to turn away from the hated present and give rein to their imagination. Such writing was also greatly encouraged by the increasing use of a popular written language (*pai-hua*) instead of the classical language of the scholars.

The best-known work to have survived from this time is *The Romance of the Three Kingdoms*, a historical novel set in the adventurous days after the downfall of the Han Dynasty in the third century A.D. Others of somewhat later date are: *All Men are Brothers,* a swashbuckling tale of bandits and adventurers; and *Record of a Journey to the West,* a light-hearted account of a Buddhist pilgrimage (translated by Arthur Waley as *Monkey*). Most of these were not written down in their present form until at least the sixteenth or seventeenth century, but their inspiration and their style are that of the Mongol era.

After Kublai Khan's death in 1294, aged eighty, the Yüan Dynasty declined. None of his successors had his ability, and their reigns were short. Moreover, the Mongol empire was too vast, and the problems of the conquered territories too different, to remain indefinitely under a single ruler. Genghiz Khan himself had granted extensive pasture lands to each of his four sons by his first wife, so that they could maintain their princely state, although the towns and settled places in these areas remained directly under the Great Khan. The natural tendency of these separate fiefs to become independent was hastened after the death of Guyuk Khan (Ogodai's son, and Genghiz' grandson) by disputes over the succession. By the time of Kublai, the suzerainty of the Great Khan over the three western divisions of the empire was largely nominal. And, while the Mongols in China were adapting themselves to the Chinese way of life, ruling according to Confucius and Buddha, in the Middle East they became Moslems and ruled as successors to the former Arab empire.

In China the antagonism, the mutual incomprehension, between the nomad, even with a veneer of civilization, and the settled, urban Chinese was stronger than ever. In Chinese eyes the Mongols remained savages who drank fermented mare's milk and wore sheepskins, who seldom washed, and who could not even speak the Chinese language.

By the middle of the fourteenth century a number of rival leaders had risen to power in the Middle Kingdom, and men watched to see who would win the Mandate of Heaven. Secret societies played a great part at this time. The White Lotus Society, reputedly dating from the fourth century, was perhaps the most powerful influence throughout the country.

The signal for the rebellion against the Mongols in 1368 was ingeniously concealed in the Moon Cakes which are traditionally exchanged between friends and neighbors on the fifteenth day of the eighth month of the year. This, the Moon's Birthday, is said to be the only day in the year when the moon is really round (corresponding to our Harvest Moon), and the Moon Cakes are dumplings stuffed with spices, melon seeds, and orange peel. A small square of paper, with a lucky inscription, is pasted on the outside of the cakes. It was thus that orders for the people in the capital to rise at a given time and massacre the Mongol soldiers who were billeted on each household were sent freely from house to house, under the eyes of the Mongols themselves.

The revolt was completely successful. The Mongols were driven out of China into the deserts from whence they came, and a new dynasty, the Ming (Brilliant), was established by one Chu Yüan-chang. Chu Yüan-chang, like the founder of the Han Dynasty fifteen hundred years before, was a man of humble birth, uncouth, an unlikely Son of Heaven, but a natural leader. By 1382 he had united China. And, although the Ming Dynasty, like the Sung, turned in upon itself and never looked far beyond its own borders, it survived and prospered for almost three hundred years. It was the last native dynasty to rule China.

12

Korea

THE CHINESE *Book of History* describes a conversation among three Shang noblemen shortly before the overthrow of that dynasty by the Chou about 1027 B.C.

"Now is the time of Shang's calamity," one lamented. "I will arise and share in its ruin. When ruin overtakes Shang, I will not be the servant of another."

True to his vow, this prince later went into exile. According to Korean legend, he crossed into northern Korea with several thousand followers, among whom were scholars, doctors, and teachers, and founded the state of Chosen (in Chinese, Ch'ao-hsien, or Morning Calm). He thus brought civilization to a land formerly barbaric, which his descendants continued to rule for nearly a thousand years.

Chosen is the first state we know of in the Korean peninsula, and it was strongly influenced by China. The only evidence for its being of such antiquity, however, rests on the *Book of History*, a somewhat dubious source. It seems, in fact, to have come into being about the third century B.C.

Korea is a large peninsula jutting from the land mass of northeast Asia into the sea midway between China and Japan. On a clear day the Japanese island of Tsushima is visible from the extreme southeast of the peninsula; the Chinese coast is only a hundred and twenty miles away across the Yellow Sea. Korea is thus a natural crossroads, a bridge between China and Japan, yet also open to the nomad lands of Manchuria, Mongolia, and central Asia. The kingdoms of northern Korea often included parts of what is now Manchuria, while the south was linked with China or Japan across the sea.

The natural boundaries of Korea are nevertheless clear: the sea on three sides, and on the north the Yalu River and a high mountain range, the highest peak of which is over 9,000 feet. Much of the peninsula itself is mountainous, and the wild, rocky nature of the land has had a great influence on its mythology, religion, and art. The west of the country is the more open, and includes more good natural harbors, so that the west has always been more in touch with the outside world. Korea has always looked toward China and has often been closely linked with her great neighbor.

In race and in language, however, the Koreans are closer to the people of northeastern and central Asia. Their ancestors, probably of Tungusic or Mongol stock, are believed to have moved south into the peninsula in waves, from about the third millennium B.C. Traces of Neolithic settlements are found throughout Korea, and their Neolithic pottery is more like that of northeast Asia than that of China. Their early religion, too, seems to have been related to shamanism (a religion in which the shamans, or priests, are believed to be able to approach and to influence the gods) and the animal worship of Siberia and northern Asia.

Chinese influence became dominant in the fourth and third centuries B.C. The Chou Dynasty had then disintegrated into the Warring States, and one of these, Yen, expanded into southern Manchuria and northern Korea. There they established the principality of Chosen. When Yen itself was overthrown by Ch'in about 240 B.C., this new state also theoretically fell to Ch'in, but it remained very much on the fringe of empire, too remote to be directly controlled. Under Ch'in Shih Huang Ti, and in the years of chaos which followed his death, many Chinese therefore took refuge in Chosen, and they undoubtedly contributed to the spread of Chinese culture in the peninsula.

During the early years of the Han Dynasty, Emperor Kao Tsu (Liu Pang) had too many other problems on his hands to think about Korea. About 195 B.C., however, a Chinese adventurer named Wei Man (in Korean, Wiman) crossed the Yalu River into Chosen with some thousand followers and begged refuge at the court of its king. He was granted land on the western frontier of the kingdom, which he promised to defend against attack, but on the flimsy pretext of an imaginary Chinese invasion he very soon marched upon the capital, deposed the king, and took the throne.

Wei Man, usurper though he was, was an able ruler. He extended the boundaries of Chosen, bringing some southern parts of the peninsula under his control. And for the time being the Chinese recognized his kingdom as at least semi-independent, a useful shield against the barbarians of the south and the northeast.

Except when she herself was expanding, China's policy was always to "protect the hedges"—that is, to keep friendly buffer states between herself and the barbarians. This was her major interest in Korea from the beginning. She also tried to keep certain areas under her influence by building local walls. The Liaotung peninsula, for instance, where China, Manchuria, and Korea meet, seems to have been protected by a wall of some kind even before the third century B.C., for we hear of Ch'in Shih Huang Ti ordering the wall there repaired. Later the peninsula was enclosed by the "Willow Fence," consisting of a ditch and an embankment; the embankment was thickly planted with willows, and these formed an effective barrier against cavalry.

Under Han Wu Ti, China turned again to conquest. We have seen how that emperor, in his efforts to outflank the Hsiung-nu, had pushed so far west that his empire almost touched that of Rome. In Korea, in 109 B.C., he took advantage of an incident when the ruler refused to come to the Chinese court and pay him homage, to invade the country. By the following year Chosen had ceased to exist. In its place Han Wu Ti set up several colonies, called commanderies, and later reduced these to a single colony occupying the northwest of the Korean peninsula.

Lo-lang, as this commandery was called, was comparable to the Roman colonies in Britain and elsewhere or, for that matter, to colonies generally, ancient or modern. The native Koreans had little to say in the matter of government, and were looked down upon by their masters. There was a definite gulf between the Chinese rulers and the subject people. Yet colonization brought the Koreans great benefits, and in the long run undoubtedly made it easier for them to become a nation, united, independent, with a background of Chinese culture which they had absorbed and made their own.

That the Chinese colonists lived an extremely comfortable life is shown by the contents of the tombs they left behind them in north Korea, dating from the second century B.C. to the third century A.D. Among their tomb furniture were lacquered bowls, baskets, trays, and tables; bronze mirrors; combs, hairpins, gold filigree ornaments, and make-up boxes for holding several different cosmetics. There were also, as in China, pottery models of just about everything a man or a woman might be expected to want in the next world.

Lo-lang remained a Chinese colony until 313 A.D., long after the Han Dynasty itself had fallen. It was only when the barbarians who overran north China at the beginning of the fourth century disrupted communications between the commandery and the Middle Kingdom that the Chinese were finally driven out.

Meanwhile, in the greater part of the peninsula, where the Chinese writ did not run, the various Korean tribes had gradually formed three native states: Koguryo, Paekche, and Silla. (These states all claimed to have been founded in the first century B.C., beginning with Silla in 57 B.C., although they did not exercise any power until several centuries later.) Koguryo, in the north, already included a part of modern Manchuria, and it now fell heir to what had been the colony of Lo-lang; it was the largest and, at least in the beginning, the most politically and culturally advanced of the three states. It was also the most belligerent. Paekche, in the southwest, was fertile and densely populated, and it had contact with China by sea, but it was militarily weak. Silla, in the southeast, was the most remote and most backward of the states. It was the last to become a kingdom, and it long retained its tribal govern-

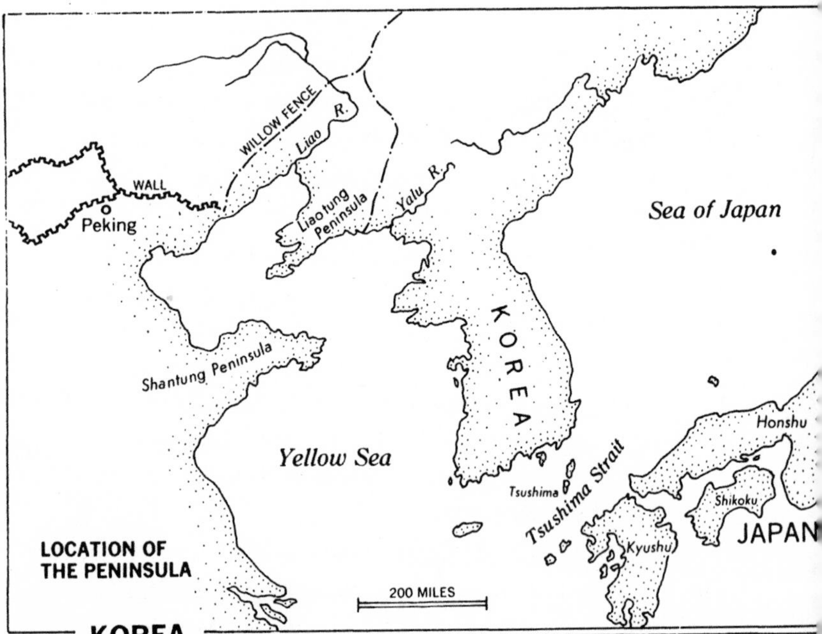
WILLOW FENCE
Liao R.
WALL
Peking
Liaotung Peninsula
Yalu R.
Sea of Japan
KOREA
Shantung Peninsula
Yellow Sea
Honshu
Tsushima
Tsushima Strait
Shikoku
JAPAN
Kyushu
LOCATION OF THE PENINSULA
200 MILES

KOREA

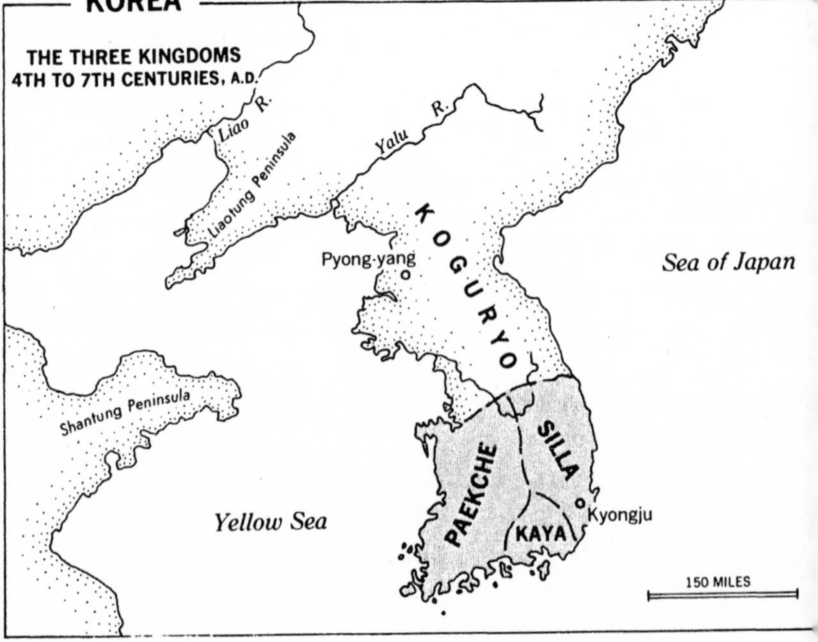
THE THREE KINGDOMS 4TH TO 7TH CENTURIES, A.D.
Liao R.
Yalu R.
Liaotung Peninsula
KOGURYO
Pyong-yang
Sea of Japan
Shantung Peninsula
Yellow Sea
PAEKCHE
SILLA
KAYA
Kyongju
150 MILES

ment, with a leader chosen by a council of the tribes, and a rigid class system—called "Bone Ranks" because it depended entirely on heredity. Yet this was its strength as well as its weakness; Silla was one day to rule the whole of Korea.

Koguryo, Paekche, and Silla, called the Three Kingdoms in imitation of the Chinese Three Kingdoms (third century A.D.), controlled almost the entire peninsula for 350 years, from the fourth to the seventh century. Hundreds of tombs dating from this time have been found, especially in Koguryo; and although the tomb furniture has long since been stolen or destroyed, the wall paintings—of flying angels, mythical animals, and flower patterns—are magnificent.

The exception to the rule of the Three Kingdoms was a small enclave in the south, Kaya (called Mimana by the Japanese), which maintained its independence and was allied with Japan, across the sea. The Kaya people may well have been kinsmen of tribes which had earlier migrated to Japan and thus related to the Japanese by blood. In any case the alliance was useful to both sides, for it gave the Japanese a foothold on the mainland, which they held until late in the sixth century, while Kaya could call on the Japanese for help when threatened by her more powerful neighbors.

It was now that Buddhism came to Korea. It came from China, reaching Koguryo about 372 A.D. Officially, at least, it quickly replaced the local nature worship and ancestor worship, and by the end of the fourth century it was recognized as the state religion. Several Buddhist monasteries were built near P'yongyang, the capital of Koguryo, and Korean pilgrims, like their Chinese counterparts, were soon traveling across cen-

A dragon. Wall painting from a tomb near P'yongyang, of the Koguryo Kingdom of Korea (6th or 7th century)

tral Asia in search of enlightenment. Nor were the other kingdoms far behind. In 384 the King of Paekche sent to China asking for monks to come and instruct them in the faith. Within the next fifty years Buddhist teachers had reached even remote Silla.

At the beginning of the seventh century China, reunited under the Sui Dynasty, determined to bring at least north Korea under her control once more. The King of Koguryo obligingly provided a pretext by raiding the Liaotung peninsula, between China and Koguryo, and the Sui Emperor protested indignantly: "Although the people and the territory of the out-of-the-way kingdom of your highness are insignificant, they are just the same my people and my territory."

When this letter had no effect, he sent armies into Korea both overland and by sea, with very little success. Heavy rain made the roads impassable for the supply wagons, or even foot soldiers, while fierce storms wrecked the warships. The Chinese had eventually to withdraw, saving face only because the King of Koguryo did agree to apologize for the raid on Liaotung. The Sui Emperor Yang Ti thereupon ordered the King to come to the Chinese court and do homage in person. The King, perhaps wisely, refused, and Yang Ti mounted a major expedition against the peninsula in 612.

Once again the Chinese met with fierce resistance. A force said to have been 300,000 strong nevertheless pushed on to within sixty-five miles of P'yongyang. There, with victory at least possible, they were met by a humble note from the King of Koguryo agreeing unconditionally to accept Chinese rule; and this persuaded them to turn back. No sooner had they begun their retreat, however, than the troops of Koguryo, hidden in the hills on either side of their route, fell upon the unsuspecting Chinese soldiers and massacred almost the entire army.

Campaigns mounted by Yang Ti in 613 and 614, although on a smaller scale, were equally disastrous, and were indeed, as we have seen, one of the main causes of the fall of the Sui Dynasty.

It is clear that, in spite of the peaceful title Land of Morning Calm, the Koreans were never a meek or easily governed people. They liked to rule themselves. The kings of Koguryo, especially, were past masters at the art of submitting to China just enough, and just at the right time, to appear as humble clients, and promptly reasserting their independence when the Chinese withdrew. The Chinese, for their part, even when fighting them, recognized the Koreans as reasonably civilized people, not barbarians. T'ang T'si Tsung described Korea as "a country of educated gentlemen."

During the sixth century, Silla, the remote kingdom in the southeast, had become increasingly pro-Chinese. She had also become increasingly powerful. Chinese strategy accordingly turned to the idea of an alliance with Silla which would enable the allies to conquer the rest of Korea. In 660, under T'ang T'ai Tsung's successor (dominated by the formidable Empress Wu) and with the help of Silla, the Chinese invaded and overwhelmed the kingdom of Paekche. In 663, again with the help of Silla, they defeated a Japanese fleet which was sailing to the aid of Paekche, a victory so decisive that it was almost a thousand years before Japan again played any major part in Korean history. Finally, in 668, Silla and the Chinese forces together defeated Koguryo.

Whether the T'ang rulers had intended to hold Korea, and were thwarted by geography and by the unexpected strength of Silla, or whether they only wanted to establish a stable government there, they soon withdrew from the peninsula. Korea, politically united for the first time as the kingdom of Silla, maintained her independence. By then the boundaries of the kingdom were essentially those of modern Korea. In fact, few nations of today can claim to have preserved for so long, so nearly unchanged, the same boundaries, the same culture, and approximately the same population.

Silla took T'ang China as her model in all things. Buddhism had already brought with it Chinese styles in art; now Chinese ceremonies were introduced at court, and Confucian principles were adopted. Well-to-do Koreans sent their sons to study at the university in Ch'ang-an. So deep was the influence at this time that even in modern Korea *Tang* is still used as a prefix for things Chinese.

Silla's capital at Kyongju, in the southeast, was modeled on Ch'ang-an. It was a city of great beauty, its gates, temples, bell towers, and palaces comparable to those of the Chinese capital, on a more modest scale. Outside the city, too, there were Buddhist monasteries, temples, and pagodas in Chinese style, richly furnished. The sculpture and bas-reliefs of this time, especially those of Sokkuram, a grotto which stands high among the hills some little distance from the capital, looking out across the eastern sea, are among the finest Buddhist works of art anywhere in the world.

Although they so faithfully imitated the Chinese, Korean art has a feeling of its own. Perhaps there is

Two Boddhisatvas. Sculpture in the Sokkuram grotto near Kyongju, Korea (Kingdom of Silla: 8th century)

an underlying North Asian influence; perhaps it is simply an individual Korean style, expressing itself in spite of attempts to be Chinese. It has great strength and realism. Korean potters, in particular, had a remarkable understanding of their material and a great sense of form. Korean celadon pottery, which was most highly developed in the time of Koryo (immediately following Silla), had a depth of color quite different from, and possibly superior to, that of the Chinese.

The only form of writing known in early Korea was Chinese, which bears no relation whatever to the spoken language; the latter belongs to the Altaic group of languages widely found in northern Asia. Korean literature could be written only in Chinese. During the seventh and eighth centuries a system was developed giving phonetic values to certain Chinese characters, thus making it possible to express Korean words in Chinese writing, but this was never widely used. Almost all literature until about the fifteenth century continued to be in Chinese.

The age of Silla, roughly contemporary with T'ang China, was a golden, peaceful age, with religion and art more important than politics or war. It was perhaps too peaceful, so that its people lost their original vitality. Or perhaps the same dynastic cycle that seems to operate in China also swung full circle in Korea. After two centuries the kingdom began to disintegrate, and in 935 a descendant of the kings of ancient Koguryo founded a new dynasty, one which was to rule Korea for 450 years. This was Koryo (a shortened version of Koguryo), the name that we have turned into Korea.

Koryo carried on close relations with China and was much influenced by the brilliant culture of the Sung

Dynasty. Yet there may have been a feeling that Chinese ways were being copied too slavishly. In 982 an adviser to the King of Koryo was writing: "Let us follow China in poetry, history, music, ceremony, and the five relationships [of Confucius], but in riding and dressing let us be Koreans."

China herself was no longer so powerful. The Sung Dynasty might be resplendent in the south, but north China was falling into the hands of one barbarian people after another, and these inevitably came into conflict with Korea. The Koreans, their land communications with China cut off, were forced to pay tribute to the northern rulers, sending annual gifts of cloth, gold, silk, and ginseng (a root, believed to have remarkable medicinal properties, for which Korea is famous).

The Khitan (Liao) Dynasty and the Juchen (Chin) Dynasty were content to leave Korea alone as a tributary state. Not so the Mongols. In 1231 they invaded Korea, besieged the Koryo capital at Songdo (modern Kaesong), and forced the Korean government to flee for their lives. The Koryo rulers succeeded in setting up a temporary capital on an island off the west coast of the peninsula, from which the Mongols were unable to dislodge them, and they held this island fortress for over twenty-five years. The Mongols, meanwhile, occupied and ravaged mainland Korea at will.

This tragic interval has one extraordinary accomplishment to its credit. Some 200 years earlier the Koreans had printed the whole of the Tripitaka, or sacred books of Buddhism, but the blocks from which they did the printing were destroyed during the Mongol invasions. Now, on their island refuge, the Buddhist monks set out to make a complete new printing. To this end they cut 81,258 hardwood blocks, each 27 by 8 inches, and each double-surfaced so that in printing they produced 162,516 pages. The labor involved was enormous (it is said to have taken fifteen years), but what is more remarkable is the accuracy of the cutting. Prints taken from the plates in recent years are apparently as good as anything that could be produced by modern offset methods. What is equally remarkable is that these blocks have survived in good condition; they are still kept in a monastery in southern Korea.

In 1258 the rulers of Koryo, unable to hold out forever, surrendered to the Mongols. Thereafter they became little more than puppets. They married Mongol princesses and spent almost all their time at the Mongol capital of Khanbaligh (Peking). By the time the Mongols were finally driven out of north China, in the fourteenth century, the Korean ruling family was almost more Mongol than Korean. The country meanwhile had suffered heavily from the Mongol occupation, and its people had been forced to provide ships, soldiers, and provisions for the two unsuccessful Mongol invasions of Japan in 1274 and 1281.

It was not until the end of the fourteenth century that a new leader arose to rescue the country from the miseries of foreign rule, invasion, and civil war, and from the struggle between pro-Mongol and pro-Chinese factions. This was Yi Song-gye, a man of remarkable military and political ability. Having seized the capital, he usurped the throne in 1392 and founded the Yi Dynasty, restoring the ancient name of Chosen to Korea. The kingdom he established was to survive for over 500 years, bringing Korea into the twentieth century.

13

Japan—the Beginning

THERE ARE STRIKING DIFFERENCES, geographically, between China and Japan. Where China is continental, with land frontiers on three sides, and did not become a seafaring country until late in her history, Japan is an island—or, rather, an archipelago—and inevitably much influenced by the sea. China has several rivers deep enough to be navigable and long enough to be useful for communication between different parts of the country. The rivers of Japan are too small to be navigable any distance inland. Central China consists of vast open plains, with fertile soil, easy to cultivate, whereas Japan is so mountainous that only about a fifth of the country is suited to agriculture. Even this consists of small coastal plains, or narrow valleys, separated from one another by hills and mountain ranges.

Central Japan enjoys damper, somewhat milder weather than north China. Both countries, however, have an extreme range of temperature. And one must remember that Japan, although a comparatively small country, stretches from north to south over a wide latitude, so that northern Hokkaido is Siberian in climate while the southern islands are warm and wet, ideal for rice cultivation.

The position of Japan as an island lying off the

shores of a great continent is sometimes compared to that of Britain. The distance between Britain and Europe, however, is far less than that between Japan and the nearest point on the Korean coast, let alone China. Until recently, Japan has been one of the most isolated countries in the world. Its civilization developed late, extraordinarily late by comparison with the Chinese mainland. For whereas Chinese cultural influences flowed into Korea by land, they moved only slowly and indirectly across the Straits of Japan, and there was little direct contact between China and Japan until the fifth or sixth century A.D.

It is still uncertain who the ancestors of the Japanese were. Physically, they are closest to the Mongoloid races. They may well have come in successive waves of migration out of northeast Asia, by way of Korea, but there was undoubtedly an early admixture of islanders from the South Pacific as well. A legend which tells how one of the gods, seeing that there was a surplus of land in southern Korea, broke off a bit of that peninsula and carried it across the straits to add on to Japan, must surely refer to Korean immigration. Other tales tell of Chinese sailors who were blown off course and landed in Japan, and of expeditions from China which never returned—such as the one sent out by Emperor Ch'in Shih Huang Ti in the third century B.C. These people were probably among the early colonists of Japan.

Whoever the settlers may have been, the ancestors of the Japanese we know now, they drove out, gradually and against considerable opposition, an earlier race whom they found there. These were the Ainu, a people whose descendants survive, although precariously, in the northernmost Japanese island of Hokkaido. The Ainu are believed to be of Caucasian stock; at least their features are European rather than Japanese, and they are hairier than other Orientals.

The earliest culture of which traces are found in Japan is called the Jomon, which goes back to about the third millennium B.C. The Jomon people lived by hunting and fishing, using implements of bone and wood, and chipping and polishing stone; they made pottery by hand, ornamenting it with a characteristic corded pattern (Jomon = Rope design), but they had apparently no knowledge of agriculture. These may have been the ancestors of the Ainu. They were followed, in about the third century B.C., by the Yayoi culture, whose people knew the use of iron and bronze, planted rice, built houses with thatched roofs, and shaped their pottery upon a wheel. Their major settlements were along the Inland Sea, that strip of water which separates the main Japanese island of Honshu from Shikoku and Kyushu islands.

From about the second or third century A.D. the leaders of the ruling tribes, or clans, began to build great grave mounds, sometimes surrounded by a moat, over their tombs, and the period of the next three hundred years or so is usually called the Tomb Culture. The mounds are similar to Korean tombs of the same period. They are found over a wide area, from Kyushu in the west through central Honshu, and among the objects unearthed from them are swords, coats of armor, and bronze mirrors.

Hollow cylinders of baked clay, called Haniwa, were often buried in these grave mounds, forming a sort of circle round the tomb. Varying considerably in size,

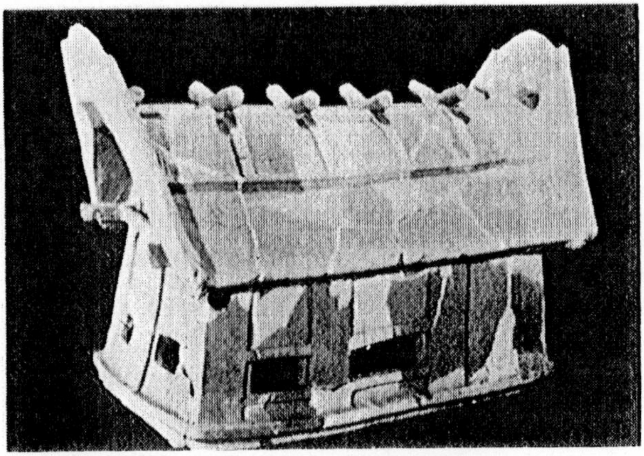

a. a house

b. a woman with a baby on her back

Haniwa tomb figures (Japanese, Period of the Tomb Culture: 3rd to early fifth centuries)

c. a man

d. a horse

the Haniwa were modeled in the shape of men and women, of warriors in suits of armor, and horses saddled, of animals both domestic and wild, as well as houses, carts, and weapons. Like the Chinese tomb figures, they have provided archaeologists with valuable information about the life of the early Japanese. They also have great charm. Their freshness and simplicity of line are extraordinarily like the best modern art.

The only records left by the peoples of the Jomon, of the Yayoi, and of the Tomb cultures alike are archaeological. There was no writing. It is thus worth looking at the legends which the Japanese themselves tell about their ancestors, the more so as, quite recently, many Japanese were still able to accept at least part of this legendary history as true. The Emperor, for instance, was assumed to be descended from the Sun Goddess, and this divinity was no vague claim nor theoretical "divine right of kings"; it was accepted as a fact.

The first of the islands of Japan was created, so it is said, when the gods Izanagi and Izanami stood on the Bridge of Heaven and stirred the water beneath them with a long, jeweled spear. As they drew this back, covered with mud, a drop of earth fell from it and formed an island. The two gods descended to the land thus created and there gave birth to innumerable other gods and to the other islands of Japan. The Sun Goddess and the Moon Goddess were later born from Izanagi's eyes when he was bathing in the sea to purify himself.

The Sun Goddess, Amaterasu, was appointed to rule the Plain of Heaven, and the Moon Goddess to rule the night. Their brother Susano-o, however, who was the wild, impetuous God of Storms, caused them so much trouble that Amaterasu finally retired into the depths of a cave. The world was left in complete darkness. Nothing would persuade her to come out again until, at last, the other gods thought of setting up a mirror outside the entrance to the cave; then they brought a cock, whose crowing made it sound as though dawn were coming, and they all began laughing, singing, and dancing. Amaterasu, curious, looked out, saw her own reflection in the mirror, and was so astonished that she stepped forward. Thus sunlight was restored to heaven and earth.

The Storm God was exiled from Heaven for his part in this quarrel. He came down to earth in Korea and, according to legend, he crossed from there to the province of Izumo, on the west coast of Japan, in a clay boat. He brought with him the seeds of many things which grew only in Heaven, such as the cryptomeria tree, and planted them in Japan.

Later, however, the Sun Goddess decided to send her own grandson Ninigi down to earth to rule Japan. He landed on Kyushu, the southern island, carrying with him the bronze mirror which had persuaded the Sun Goddess to come out of her cave, an iron sword which the Storm God had once given her, and a curved jewel. The three symbols have remained the sacred regalia of Japanese rulers from that day to this. And Ninigi, according to one story, is directly responsible for the poor health of many Japanese emperors because, after he had descended to the earth, he insisted on marrying a beautiful but weakly girl rather than her ugly, strong sister; the father of the two girls warned him at the time that his descendants would inherit his wife's delicate constitution.

The foundation of the Japanese state is credited to the great-grandson of Ninigi, known as Jimmu Tenno. This "Divine Warrior," as he is called, is said to have led his people eastward along the Inland Sea, by water and by land, and to have established his capital in the Yamato basin, somewhere south of the modern city of Nara. This basin, a plain of perhaps two hundred square miles, is the most fertile part of Japan and the heart of early Japanese civilization.

It is not hard to see, in the stories of how one god came to Izumo by way of Korea, and another descended on a mountaintop in Kyushu, echoes of early migrations from the continent to Japan. The second, the "Sun-line," probably absorbed the Izumo settlers at a comparatively early date. And, although Jimmu Tenno may not have been the great-great-great-grandson of the Sun Goddess, and although the dates assigned to him in early Japanese records are not taken seriously, there is no reason to doubt his existence. Nor need one doubt that he led an expedition to the east. Such an expedition certainly seems to have taken place, at the expense of the Ainu, and to have established the state of Yamato. Jimmu Tenno was very likely the first of the Yamato line of rulers, possibly among those kings who built the great grave mounds of the Tomb Culture.

We should not think of the Yamato "emperors" as ruling in the same way that the Chinese Sons of Heaven did, from at least the time of Ch'in Shih Huang Ti. They were the leaders of a particular clan, little if any more powerful than the leaders of other clans. Until the end of the seventh century the various clans governed their own people, ruled their own lands, and were politically independent. The "Emperor," divine descendant of Amaterasu, was a sort of high priest, presiding over the religious ceremonies for them all, but he did not necessarily combine this with any great temporal power.

The early religion of Japan had no name until the coming of Buddhism, in the sixth century, when it was given the (originally Chinese) name Shinto (the Way of the Gods) to distinguish it from the new faith (Butsudo, the Way of the Buddhas). It was not, and never has been, a religion in the same sense as the great religions of the world, for it had no founder nor any great teacher comparable to Christ, Buddha, or Mohammed. It has no Bible nor Koran. Nor is it a way of life in the Confucian sense. It is perhaps closest to the Greek and Roman belief in household gods and gods of the fields, forests, and mountains—the feeling that all things are, in some sense, alive.

Shinto may be called nature worship to the extent that divinity is recognized, and worshiped, in natural objects. Certain things which may be exceptionally beautiful or exceptionally useful, of great age or of peculiar shape, are called Kami, meaning "superior" and often translated as "god" or "spirit." A waterfall or a spring or a tree, a rock or a stone—especially boundary stones between fields—may have Kami. Tools or weapons, an inkstand or a writing brush, may have Kami. So may certain people: ancient heroes, men of great courage, and one's own ancestors. But whereas the Greeks and Romans tended to personify their spirits of nature, to think of dryads dwelling in the trees and nymphs in the waterfall, the Kami retained their natural shape. A stone was a stone, even if animated by a divine spirit; it was honored, worshiped, but not turned into a god by being clothed in man's own image.

The Yamato period, beginning about the third century A.D., was one of conquest and adventure. In the early days it is difficult to distinguish fact from fancy. The great legendary hero of the time was Yamato Dake, or the Brave of Yamato, a prince who—if he existed—may have lived during the fourth century. Yamato Dake is credited with having driven back the "barbarians" both to the east and west of the newly established Yamato state. Many of his adventures, his encounters with unfriendly deities in animal disguise, and the story of how his wife threw herself into the sea to calm the waters and thus saved his life, belong to folklore. Yet the expansion of Yamato and the conquests east and west did take place, and behind them there may well have been some such heroic figure as Yamato Dake, a figure in many ways comparable to King Arthur.

The same is true of the Empress Jingo. Jingo was the wife of Yamato Dake's son, and she is said to have conquered Korea. Her fleet crossed the sea on the crest of a great tidal wave, which so terrified the Korean ruler that he surrendered at once, swearing allegiance until such time as the sun should rise in the west and set in the east, until rivers flowed upward from the sea, and until pebbles rose from earth to heaven and became stars. One result of the campaign was that the son she bore soon after returning to Yamato, who could thus be said to have shared in the invasion, was centuries later deified as the God of War.

Empress Jingo's conquest may have some historical foundation. The little enclave of Kaya, or Mimana, on the south coast of Korea, which was so closely allied with Japan, dates back to at least the fourth century. Early contacts between the two countries are taken for granted, and Japanese pirates undoubtedly raided the Korean coast during those centuries. As for the "conquest" being credited to a woman, women, beginning with the Sun Goddess, played an important part in early Japanese history. The first reliable mention of Japan in Chinese records calls it the Queen Country.

These early records are the annals of Wei, northernmost of the Chinese Three Kingdoms (220–265/280 A.D.), and they were written in the third century. The Japan they describe would be somewhere between the Yayoi and the Tomb cultures, before or in the early days of the Yamato period. They tell of embassies from the Queen Country traveling to the court of a Chinese governor stationed in Korea, and of Chinese who paid return visits to Japan. They describe a settled society, divided into a number of clans or tribes, living mainly by agriculture and fishing—a society already marked by definite class distinctions, and extremely law-abiding.

After the fall of the kingdom of Wei there is no mention of Japan in Chinese records for over a century, although contacts between Japan and Korea certainly continued. Then, in the fifth century, Chinese records mention several embassies from Japan coming to visit the court of the Liu Sung Dynasty (420–476) in south China. By that time the Yamato rulers would have been well established in central Japan.

The beginning of the fifth century saw the beginning of accurate historical records in Japan itself. Until then, although the Chinese script must have been known and used by individual Japanese, there was no official writing in Japan. From about 400 A.D., however, Korean scholars from Paekche were employed by the Japanese rulers to keep their official court records in Chinese script.

It may seem odd that Korean scribes should record Japanese history in Chinese writing. The spoken languages of China and Japan have nothing in common, nor is Chinese writing in the least suited to the Japanese language. Yet it shows the relation between the countries at that time. China, already so advanced, so powerful, so much larger, was beginning to exercise such an attraction on Japan that it was quite natural for the latter, being in need of a written language, which she did not yet possess, to adopt that of her great neighbor. It was equally natural that the first scribes should be Korean, for Korea was the bridge across which Chinese civilization entered Japan. (The Japanese later developed a script of their own, but they continued to use Chinese characters as well. Educated Japanese can still read Chinese today, although the spoken languages remain entirely different.)

After writing, the most important element of Chinese civilization to reach Japan was Buddhism. Again, it came by way of Korea. In 552 A.D. the king of Paekche sent the ruler of Japan copies of various Buddhist scriptures, a gilt-bronze statue of the Buddha, and a letter recommending the new religion as the most excellent of all doctrines. Despite this, it met with considerable opposition, partly because it seemed to threaten Shinto and the worship of the Sun Goddess, partly because the clans who opposed it realized that, if Buddhism were accepted, the influence of their rivals, who supported it, would be enormously increased.

The struggle was thus as much political as religious. The more conservative Japanese clans were against the new religion, while others, especially the clan of Soga, were strongly in favor. The Sogas embraced Buddhism from the very beginning and clung to it in the face of fierce opposition and persecution. Its final victory was a victory for the Soga family. Strengthening their position by intermarriage with the imperial clan, the Sogas controlled the government for the next half century.

Whereas, before then, Chinese culture had been filtering gradually into Japan, the borrowing now became conscious and on a large scale. The leader in this deliberate opening up of Japan to Chinese civilization was Prince Shotoku, an ardent Buddhist and a man of great ability. Shotoku set the pattern for centuries to come. He sent embassies to the court of the Sui Dynasty, and these received a friendly welcome, although there was some friction when the Empress of Japan referred to herself as Ruler of the Land of the Rising Sun and to the Emperor Yang Ti as Ruler of the Land of the Setting Sun. Sui Yang Ti was not one to accept anyone as his equal, and certainly not the female ruler of a people whom he regarded as "eastern barbarians."

These embassies to the court of Sui, and later to that of T'ang, were not concerned simply with diplomacy or with trade. They included many young men sent to study mathematics, law, astronomy, music, literature, painting, Buddhism, Confucianism, and the Chinese state. Some of these men stayed for years, even a generation. On their return they became the leaders of a new Japan.

Whatever was Chinese was readily adopted, whether in politics, science, or manners. The Chinese system of a central government with a supreme ruler officially replaced the old system of clans, in which the Emperor was only one among a number of tribal rulers. "A country does not have two lords; the people do not have two masters," Shotoku is quoted as saying.

One exception to this universal adoption of things Chinese was the examination system. As in Korea, the hereditary principle, the class system, was so strongly entrenched that, although universities of higher learning were set up, they were reserved for the sons of noble families. Only in China, far ahead of her time, could ability and intelligence be rewarded regardless of rank, and important government posts filled by open, competitive examination.

Buddhism meanwhile had overcome all opposition. It filled a need for color and movement which the austere ceremonies of Shinto did not provide. It brought with it an entirely new world, a world of beauty. It is not too much to say that the love and appreciation of beauty in all its forms has been one of the strongest characteristics of the Japanese ever since that time. Sculpture, architecture, and painting were called upon to serve the new religion, and the sudden, brilliant flowering of Japanese art in the seventh and eighth centuries was almost entirely inspired by Buddhism.

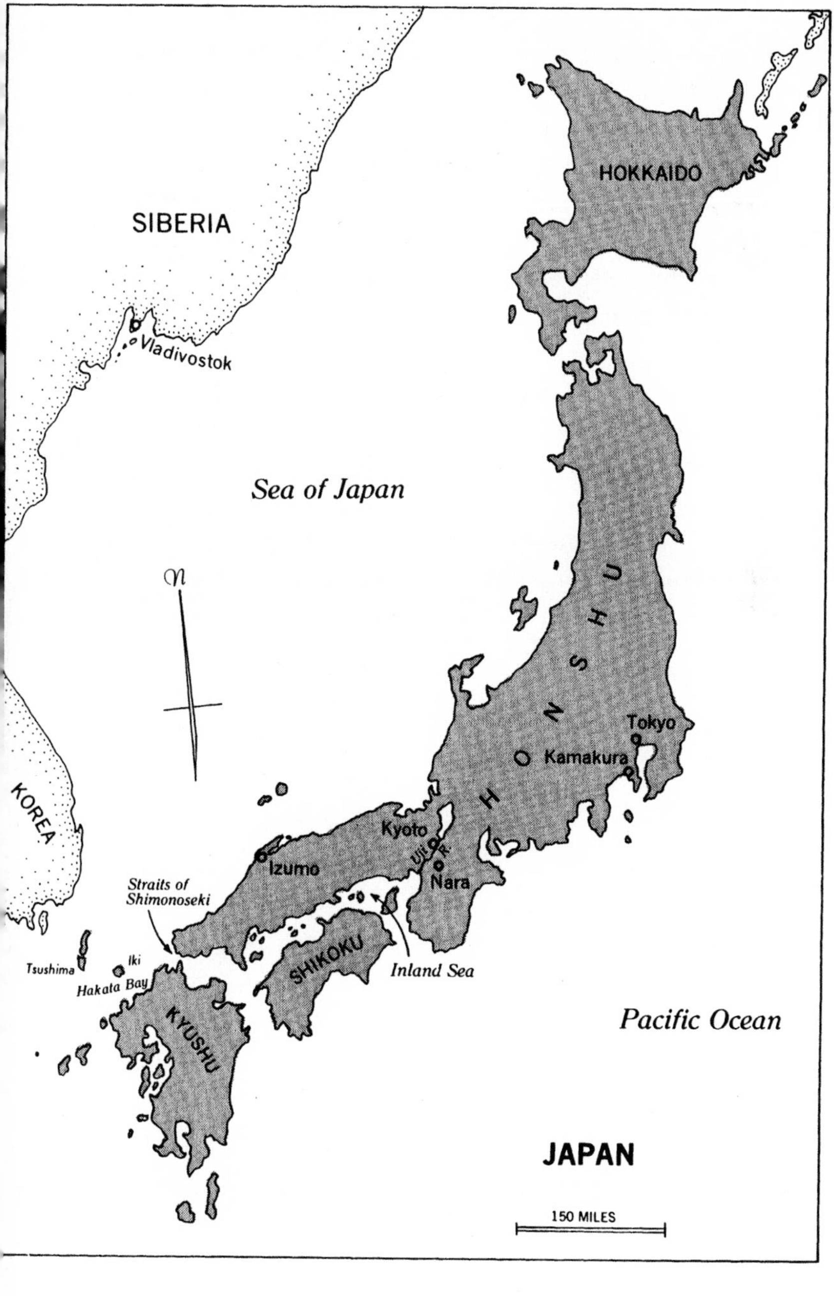
SIBERIA
HOKKAIDO
Vladivostok
Sea of Japan
HONSHU
Tokyo
Kamakura
KOREA
Kyoto
Uji R.
Nara
Izumo
Straits of Shimonoseki
Tsushima
Iki
Hakata Bay
SHIKOKU
Inland Sea
KYUSHU
Pacific Ocean
JAPAN
150 MILES

It did not replace Shintoism. The two religions existed side by side, and it was perfectly possible for a man to follow the simple worship of the old gods and yet accept the new. Confucianism also had its place. The Taika reforms, which were introduced from 645 on, and which were meant to strengthen and centralize government control of the country, were based on Confucian principles. Shotoku himself, the ardent Buddhist, had a Confucian tutor.

Shotoku marked the break between old Japan and a new level of culture. It had needed the spark of Chinese civilization to set it alight. For a time it would still depend on direct, often uncritical, imitation of China, but by the end of the ninth century this had come to an end, and Japan was developing her own distinctive style of life and culture.

14

Nara and Heian-Kyo

The early Japanese were not great builders. They did not instinctively think in terms of cities, enclosed within walls, as the Chinese did from the beginning. Cities scarcely existed in Japan before the eighth century. The capital of the country was wherever the ruling emperor's palace happened to be; and, as a result, it changed from reign to reign, though usually remaining in some part of the Yamato basin.

In 695, however, it was decided to build a capital city modeled on the great T'ang capital of Ch'ang-an. The first experimental planned capital seems not to have been successful, and it was abandoned in 710 for a new city, also modeled on Ch'ang-an. It was smaller, of course, but it was laid out on exactly the same plan, oriented to the points of the compass, with the emperor's residence at the north.

This was Nara. It must have been a city of remarkable beauty, a symbol of the transformation now taking place in Japanese culture—a transformation inspired indeed by China but nevertheless one of the most extraordinary artistic achievements of any country at any time. The Japanese mastered the styles and techniques of T'ang art with ease and were soon producing masterpieces of their own, by no means inferior to their

A Boddhisatva. Statue in wood of the 7th Century (Horyuji temples near Nara, Japan)

models. The Nara period was the golden age of Japanese sculpture; although they worked less in stone than did the Chinese, they developed great skill in wood and bronze, and their lacquer was finer than that of China.

Nara was a city of temples. In 607, long before the capital was there, Prince Shotoku had founded the Horyuji temples nearby. These have been much restored through the years, but the original seventh-century Great Hall and the five-storied pagoda of Horyuji are

Pagoda and Main Hall of Horyuji Temple, near Nara, Japan (7th century)

still standing; they are the oldest wooden buildings in the world. Other temples and monasteries soon followed, both inside and outside the city. Japanese architecture of this period is of special interest because almost no buildings of the Sui and T'ang dynasties, which the Japanese copied, survive in China itself, and one can best imagine what they were like by studying those of Japan.

Nara remained the capital for seventy-four years, during which time Buddhist influence was very strong and the Buddhist monasteries played an increasing, not altogether beneficial part at court. This was especially so under the Empress Koken, who ruled (with a break between 758 and 764, after which she is confusingly known as Empress Shotoku) from 749 to 770.

Koken, or Shotoku, was not a particularly good ruler. She became so dominated by a certain Buddhist priest that there was danger of his usurping the throne. This may have been one reason why, after her time, women were barred from the throne. (Another reason was probably the adoption of Chinese rules of succession, for women in China did not inherit the throne.) Yet Koken has a special claim to fame. During the second half of her reign she fulfilled a vow she had made by ordering the manufacture of one million miniature clay pagodas, three and a half inches in diameter at the base and four and a half inches high. In each of these was placed a Buddhist text, printed on a narrow slip of paper about eighteen inches long, and they were then distributed among all the temples of Nara. What is remarkable about these texts, a few of which survive, is that they were printed. They are the first known examples anywhere in the world of printing from wooden blocks.

Many elements went into the invention of printing, which took place in the Orient centuries before it was known in the West. The most important of these were the invention of paper, the use of seals, and the impetus of Buddhism. Paper, as we have seen, was invented by the Chinese in the second century A.D. Seals had been employed on official documents since at least the third century B.C., and by the time of the Han Dynasty (206 B.C.–220 A.D.) they were quite common; but they were still used—as we use them in the West—to stamp impressions in soft clay or wax. With the coming of the T'ang Dynasty they were also stamped with ink on paper, like a rubber stamp, which is exactly the same principle as block printing. As for the influence of Buddhism, the advantage of printing is that it can produce any number of copies from a single block of wood, stone, or metal, as the case may be, and it was the missionary zeal of Buddhism—the wish to churn out endless copies of charms and sacred texts—that hastened the development of printing.

The first printed book still in existence, which is far more advanced in technique than the Empress Shotoku's primitive charms, is Chinese. It is a Buddhist work, printed in 868, and it was discovered about 1900 in a cave at Tun-huang, on the fringe of central Asia; preserved by the dry desert air, it is in almost perfect condition.

(This is still far from the invention of *movable* type. The Chinese did experiment with movable type made of clay, and baked, from about the eleventh century. But credit for the invention of metal type probably belongs to the Koreans, who printed a book by that means in the year 1409. The introduction to this book explains that the King of Korea, observing that it was impossible to print all existing books from solid blocks, ordered "that characters be formed of bronze, and that everything without exception upon which I can lay my hands be printed, in order to pass on the tradition of what these works contain. That will be a blessing to all eternity." Thus the first font of metal type was cast in Korea half a century before Gutenberg's "invention" of printing from movable type in Europe.)

The domination of the Nara government by powerful Buddhist monasteries may have been one reason why the imperial clan decided to move the capital from there. In 794 a new capital was established in a more strategic position, and one where the *feng-shui* was better. (*Feng-shui,* literally wind-water, is the Chinese name for a pseudo-scientific theory according to which the natural features of a site, the hills and lakes nearby, the direction of the wind, the points of the compass, and so forth make it lucky or unlucky.) This new city was Heian-Kyo, which we may call by its more familiar name, Kyoto. And whether or not it was due to the favorable *feng-shui,* it remained the capital of Japan, at least in name, until 1868.

Modeled again on Ch'ang-an, the city was a rectangle, its streets laid out at regular intervals, and the important avenues numbered from One to Nine. The Imperial Palace and its Great Enclosure, with the government offices and assembly halls, formed an inner rectangle at the north, with its own walls. From there a huge central avenue, almost a hundred yards wide and lined with willow trees, ran straight to the southern gate of the city, with markets and residential districts on both sides. The population, however, was never large enough for the city as planned, and by the tenth century the western part was almost deserted. Modern Kyoto occupies, roughly, the eastern half of the original city.

In early Kyoto, as in Nara, China was the model for all things—from the structure of the government to the color of buildings in the new capital, or even the form of words in which the nobles spoke to one another. Chinese history and Chinese literature were the studies proper to an educated man. Buddhism remained powerful; and the three important Buddhist sects—Shingon, Tendai, and the Pure Land—were all influenced by China.

Shingon was founded early in the ninth century by Kobo Daishi, a remarkable man, an artist and a philosopher, who had studied for many years in Ch'ang-an; he remains the most popular saint in Japanese Buddhism today. His followers believed the entire universe to be a reflection of one Supreme Being, and this made it easy to identify popular Shinto deities and even the Sun Goddess with Buddhism, as being simply different aspects of that Being.

The Tendai sect, founded about the same time, was equally adaptable in a different way, for it taught that different levels and different views of truth could all be valid. The Pure Land sect, somewhat later, proclaimed that all a man needed to do to reach Heaven was to repeat the name of Amida Buddha over and over and over again. This, naturally, was a very popular idea.

Monks of the Pure Land sect led their disciples dancing through the streets, chanting the name of Amida, and rejoicing that salvation was within the reach of all, whether rich or poor.

With the beginning of the tenth century the official Japanese missions to China ceased, although private individuals continued to make the long, hazardous journey. Chinese culture had, of course, a continuing influence on Japan, but the period of direct copying was at an end. With increasing self-confidence the Japanese took what they liked and used it in their own way.

The Confucian pattern of government, for instance, had never been really suited to Japan, and the clans soon managed to ignore it. Whatever the reformers might say about a country having only one lord, the Japanese Emperor's position was never comparable to that of the Chinese Son of Heaven. There was no Mandate of Heaven. The virtue of the ruler had nothing to do with his being on the throne, which was his by right of descent from the Sun Goddess. He might or might not hold real power; more often he did not. But there could be no question of his being deposed. While the clan leaders fought, and ousted one another, the Imperial Japanese dynasty remained on the throne from beginning to end.

It was now that the Japanese began to use *Kana*, a new type of phonetic writing—not an alphabet but a system whereby whole syllables were represented by symbols. They could thus break away from Chinese characters and write down their own language as it was spoken, although Chinese remained the script for all official and classical writing. One curious result of this was that, whereas the men continued to write mainly in Chinese characters, the women, not having much classical education, used the new *Kana* style. It was the women who wrote the popular, lively works, the novels, the diaries that we can still enjoy today. It is no accident that the two most famous literary works of Heian-Kyo are *The Tale of Genji* by Lady Murasaki, and *The Pillow Book of Sei Shonagon,* another court lady.

The world reflected in these books seems to us almost incredible; and yet, as far as we know, they give an accurate picture of the life of the Japanese aristocracy in the tenth century. Its atmosphere is autumnal, even decadent, which is strange in such a young civilization. Although the ceremonial of the Heian court was Chinese, its life had completely lost the ebullience of early T'ang China; it was withdrawn, unreal, almost painfully exquisite. It was as insular as China was cosmopolitan. This was partly, of course, because Japan was in fact an island, with no opening to the west such as China found in central Asia; partly also because the Japanese had adopted a way of life different from their own, and it therefore became rigid—lovingly preserved but artificial.

In this ingrown world the essential thing was the appreciation of beauty. A gentleman sending a note to his beloved must use the color of paper suited to his mood, and if, as was likely, he pinned his message to a flower or a twig, it must be the right color—maple leaves with red, willow for blue. The lady's answer would be judged by her handwriting and by the skill with which she replied to her lover's poetic allusions. Morals were less important than that the shading colors in a lady's inner and outer sleeves should be correct, and a color too pale or too bright was a grave social blunder. Palace ladies were forbidden to wear more than six skirts at once, a rule not always observed; at one New Year's party the number of skirts was so excessive, the silks so heavy, that the ladies had scarcely enough strength left to lift their fans. Their hair also weighed heavily, for women prided themselves on long, glossy, straight black hair hanging, if possible, to the ground.

On ceremonial occasions the nobles rode in a procession of gorgeously decorated oxcarts, although since these carts moved at two miles an hour the celebrations must have been rather prolonged. Horse-racing, polo, and archery were popular, and there were competitions of every kind—competitions in poetry, in blending perfumes, and in painting; exhibitions of flowers and of songbirds. Everything, including religion, was viewed from an aesthetic point of view, and the robe of a priest was as important as his faith; he must be handsome, of course, for only then would people keep their eyes and minds on him while he preached. We may call this life shallow, as indeed it was, but let us remember that it was also almost without violence, and that its main quality was its constant delight in beauty.

Its background was simple and elegant. The houses were of wood—always the basic building material in Japan—and rarely more than one story high, with graceful sloping roofs and deep eaves. The floors were bare and polished. Most of life, waking or sleeping, was spent on the floor; for, although chairs were known, they were seldom used except in the palace, and bedding was spread out on the floor. Sliding shutters and doors could be pulled back to leave the rooms open to light and air. Almost every noble's house had its own walled compound, with a landscaped garden of rocks, pools, and fine white sand. The houses were raised on piles above the ground, and water from the garden was often channeled to run underneath, with miniature bridges built across miniature streams to connect the separate rooms with one another. At a festival called Winding Water guests would sit at the edge of the stream while wine cups were floated along it; and as each cup passed, the guest would lift it, drink, and recite a poem of his own composition before letting the cup drift on to the next guest. It was assumed that any man or woman could compose an appropriate, impromptu poem for any occasion.

This exquisite world was of course only a fraction of the population of Japan in the tenth and eleventh centuries—a few thousand people at most. The majority lived and worked on the land. They were poor, illiterate, highly taxed; and, as far as they were concerned, the influence of Chinese culture, the subtleties of color and form and handwriting that so delighted the aristocracy of Kyoto, might never have existed.

Even in the capital it is unlikely that the nobles spent all their time in oxcart processions moving at two miles an hour. The romantic, frivolous existence of Genji and the ladies he courted must have had another side. Officials and administrators must have kept the wheels of government running.

The court was dominated by the Fujiwara family. This had long been a powerful clan; and, after one of its members was appointed Grand Minister of State in the ninth century, it exercised control on a virtually hereditary basis. The Minister placed a grandson of his upon the throne and made himself Regent, the first regent who was not of royal blood, and the first to rule in the name of a male sovereign. It was a pattern that later became common. The Fujiwara would marry their daughters into the imperial clan; then, whenever a Fujiwara empress had a son old enough to appear at court, they would persuade the Emperor to abdicate in favor of his son, appointing a Fujiwara Regent. Violence was seldom necessary to achieve their ends. Constant intermarriage, and the power they derived from increasing ownership of land, gave them enormous political pressure.

The Fujiwara period is reckoned from 857 to 1160, although descendants of the clan played a major part at court until the nineteenth century. Some emperors, especially if they did not have Fujiwara mothers, asserted their independence, but the strength of the Fujiwara clan was such that they always returned to power. They fought, indeed, among themselves, with now one and now another branch of the family prevailing, but their struggles were not about any question of policy, of relations with China, of religion, or indeed anything except which Fujiwara should hold power.

Most Fujiwara leaders therefore seem as two-dimensional as the court around them. Yet they must have had remarkable qualities. Moreover, they maintained their loyalty to the throne throughout, and made no attempt to overthrow the imperial line, as happened so often in China.

The height of the Fujiwara power was between 995 and 1027, when Michinaga succeeded in marrying his daughters to no less than four emperors. Michinaga was the greatest of the Fujiwara, an able statesman, a shrewd judge of men, personally brave, a fine horseman, unscrupulous, and a great lover of luxury as well as power. (The character of Prince Genji may have been modeled upon him, although he must have had a greater capacity for work.) He placed emperors upon the throne almost at will. His estates were larger, his style of life more magnificent, than those of the rulers he served. Being also, of course, a poet, he did not hesitate to compare himself in verse to the full moon, flawless, shining undimmed by any cloud.

In his later years Michinaga retired to a monastery to end his life in meditation, but he saw to it that the monastery was rebuilt at great expense, to be worthy of him. The Emperor came to visit him there; and when he died there was three months' court mourning.

The convention that emperors should abdicate at an early age became further complicated toward the end of the eleventh century, when some retired emperors insisted on retaining a measure of power. There could thus be three courts and three centers of government: that of the reigning Emperor; that of his Fujiwara Regent; and that of the "Cloistered Emperor," who had already abdicated.

The delicate, hothouse world of Genji could not last forever. It was remarkable that it lasted so long. During the eleventh century the absolute predominance of the Fujiwara in the capital, and of the capital in the life of Japan, declined. Power and leadership gradually shifted to the provinces—especially to the broad, fertile eastern plain where Tokyo now stands—and to a new class of men, the aristocratic but provincial warriors, as opposed to the noblemen of the capital.

The economic gap between Kyoto and the country was decreasing. More land had been brought under cultivation, communications improved, and new industries outside the capital were becoming more important in the country's economy. Members of the great clans, even the Fujiwara, turned to the provinces to seek their fortunes. Japan, in fact, was becoming a nation rather than an effete, overcivilized court set against a background of rural poverty.

By the twelfth century a strong feudal society existed outside the capital. In theory the great estates might still belong to the Kyoto nobles, but their administration, and their defense, were in the hands of feudal lords, rapidly becoming too powerful to remain subordinate.

These lords attracted followers who were called samurai (literally, servants)—knights who served them with intense loyalty, often generation after generation. The system was not unlike that of feudal Europe in the Middle Ages. The code of the samurai, the "way of the horse and the bow," demanded absolute devotion to their lord; it also laid emphasis on generosity and uprightness of character and encouraged chivalry toward the young, the old, and the weak. If the individual samurai did not always live up to these ideals, neither did all medieval knights. A samurai was expected to kill himself rather than face dishonor, and it was rare that one hesitated to do so. The Japanese seem always to have had a tendency to suicide, and entire families would kill themselves rather than be taken prisoner by an enemy. Only samurai, however, were allowed to commit suicide by "hara-kiri," or cutting open one's own belly—a dubious privilege.

The warrior knights who were the backbone of this new military strength were no poor adventurers. Their horses and their equipment were of fine quality. Their armor consisted of small strips of steel laced together by leather thongs, light and very flexible. Their "great harness" included a helmet with neck and shoulder armor attached, extending well over the upper arm, which took the place of a shield; shields were never used, both hands being needed for either sword or bow and arrow. Their weapons were a curved sword of fine steel, cutting like a razor, and a long bow, its arrows discharged with great skill even from the back of a horse in full gallop.

The twelfth century was notable for the rivalry of two great military clans, the Taira and the Minamoto. Both were descended from former emperors and had close connections at court, and they now found themselves involved in a civil war between different factions of the Fujiwara. It would be too simple to say that the Taira supported one and the Minamoto another; some leaders changed allegiance, and Taira and Minamoto warriors occasionally found themselves on the same side. The enmity between the clans was nevertheless deep. The outcome of their struggles was to mark the end of the Heian period and the beginning of a new form of government in Japan.

15

Feudal Japan

THE GREAT STRUGGLE between the Taira and the Minamoto clans in the twelfth century can be compared to the Wars of the Roses in fifteenth-century England, and not only because the Taira fought under red banners and the Minamoto under white. Beginning as a conflict between rival Fujiwara leaders supporting rival emperors, it lasted nearly thirty years, a time of violence and heroism, treachery, chivalry, and self-sacrifice, the remembrance of which has colored Japanese literature and legend to this day.

Little quarter was asked or given. Yet the grim background of bloodshed is lightened by moments of unexpected gentleness. One poem which became famous was found rolled up inside the helmet of one of the great Taira warriors by the Minamoto who had killed him:

> "Twilight upon my path,
> And for mine inn tonight
> The shadow of a tree,
> And for mine host, a flower."

The Uji River, near Kyoto, which was the scene of many fierce battles during the war, is thought to be still haunted by the ghosts of those who died there eight hundred years ago. On the twentieth of the fourth month, anniversary of one crucial battle, swarms of fireflies are said to gather on opposite banks of the river and meet in midstream like two armies clashing head on; these are the spirits of the Taira and the Minamoto, refighting the old battles.

The first phase of the struggle ended in 1160 with a complete victory for the Taira. The Minamoto leaders were massacred almost to a man. The oldest surviving son of their chief, Yoritomo, aged fourteen, was taken prisoner and, when asked whether he wished to live or die, he replied that he would prefer life, since it was his duty to pray for the souls of his father and his elder brothers. Touched by this, the Taira spared his life and sent him into exile in the eastern provinces. It was a piece of rare and, from the point of view of the Taira, mistaken generosity, for Yoritomo was to destroy them.

The Taira ruled supreme for twenty years. They made the mistake, however, of establishing their headquarters in Kyoto, where they became identified with the court and lost touch with the country. They enjoyed and sometimes abused their power. Even in the capital their excessive arrogance turned people against them and brought them into conflict with the Cloistered Emperor of the time, Go-Shirakawa. They also antagonized the Buddhist monasteries, who now maintained powerful independent armies of their own, and who often played a destructive part in national affairs; they were dangerous enemies because to oppose them was to be accused of sacrilege.

During these years a series of natural disasters showed that Heaven also was displeased. Famine was widespread; plagues, earthquakes, and storms ravaged the capital, and fires, which were always common in a city mainly built of wood, were even more frequent and more disastrous. A sense of doom hung over Kyoto.

By 1180 Yoritomo was strong enough to take the field against his enemies. The situation was complicated by the shifting loyalties of the imperial family and of the Minamoto themselves, for Yoritomo did not always trust his kinsmen, nor they him. In 1183, however, the Cloistered Emperor Go-Shirakawa gave his

support to the Minamoto and thus enabled them to claim that they were fighting for a legitimate cause. The Taira were thrown on the defensive, and after a number of hard-fought battles they abandoned the capital and retired to the shores of the Inland Sea, where their greatest strength lay. They took with them the reigning emperor, a boy of seven or eight related to the Taira clan through his mother, and the Sacred Regalia—the mirror, the curved jewel, and the sword.

"Battle of the Uji River." Japanese screen—*Courtesy, Victoria and Albert Museum, London. Crown copyright.*

Thus they too could claim to be the legitimate government of the country.

The Taira were still strong. They were masters of the Inland Sea. They had a powerful fleet, and they occupied an apparently impregnable position along the coast, protected on the landward side by precipitous mountains, from which they planned to launch a new attack in their own good time. But the Minamoto had one great asset: their leaders, especially Yoshitsune, a younger half brother of Yoritomo, were brilliant generals. Yoshitsune now led a party of horsemen, less than a hundred strong, up the supposedly impassable mountains behind the Taira encampment. From there they charged down in a wild, completely unexpected attack, set fire to the camp, and slaughtered or took prisoner ten times their own number. What was left of the Taira army retreated, demoralized, by boat.

A year later Yoshitsune used much the same tactics to drive the Taira from their main base at Yashima, on Shikoku Island. After a swift, unobserved crossing by boat from the mainland, he set campfires blazing all across the countryside in their rear. The Taira, thinking they faced a major attack and knowing themselves to be stronger at sea, as their enemies were on land, abandoned the base altogether and set sail for the Straits of Shimonoseki two hundred miles to the west. Even had they thought of turning back when they realized what had happened, it was too late. Yoshitsune immediately occupied Yashima and made his own headquarters there, building up a fleet, and training his men for the sea, until he was ready to move west in pursuit of the enemy.

The end came on April 25, 1185, when the Taira

were overwhelmingly defeated in a great sea battle at Dan-no-ura in the Straits of Shimonoseki. They had gone bravely out to battle, trusting in their superior naval skill, but they seem to have misjudged the tide. At the end of the day their ships were forced in toward the land, where all possible retreat had been cut off by the Minamoto. The disaster was complete.

When there was no hope left, the grandmother of the young Emperor took the child into her arms and leaped from the flagship into the water. She was followed by other court ladies, carrying the Imperial Regalia, although these were later recovered by the victorious Minamoto.

Since that day strange things have happened in the treacherous waters there at the western gate of the Inland Sea. The noise of battle is often heard, without reason, and ships are believed to have been lost when the ghosts of Taira warriors rose from the sea and dragged them down. Strange lights are seen both on land and on water. An unusual species of crab, found only near Dan-no-ura, has markings on its back like a

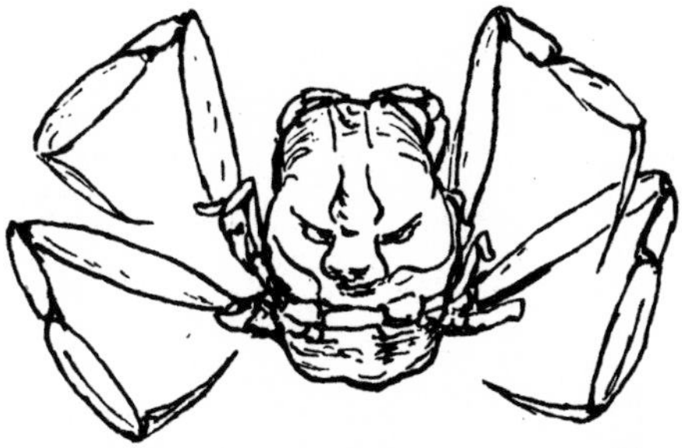

Heike crab

human face, and these are called Heike Crabs (Heike was another name for the Taira), and are thought to be the spirits of the dead.

Yoritomo's triumph marks the beginning of the feudal period. Although the capital and the imperial government remained in Kyoto, Yoritomo and his successors saw to it that their own men were in control of the great provincial estates which held the real power. Moreover, remembering the downfall of the Taira, Yoritomo made his headquarters at Kamakura, on the edge of the eastern plain, far from Kyoto, and called his government Bakufu, or Tent Government, to make it clear that authority was in the hands of the military.

In 1192 Yoritomo was appointed Sei-i Tai Shogun, or "Barbarian-quelling General," the supreme military command. From then until the mid-nineteenth century shoguns ruled the country—although always, still, in the name of the divine Emperor. It was even more indirect than this, for the Emperor was often a minor, who was advised by his father, who might be advised by his ministers, who in turn received orders from the Shogun. The remarkable thing is that the system worked.

Yoritomo was far-sighted, clear-headed, and even more skillful in politics than in war. Sansom describes him as "a truly great man, one of the greatest in Japanese history, perhaps the greatest of all if one takes into account the difficulty of his tasks and the measure of his achievements . . . the founder of a coherent system of government which, despite civil wars and other obstacles, lasted without fundamental change for centuries. He was not a mere warlord fighting for victory over rival clans. He was in a true sense a revolutionary

Minamoto Yoritomo (12th century portrait)

leader, determined to alter the constitution of the State."

He was, however, jealous of all rivals, especially those of his own blood. By the time he died, aged fifty-two, only fourteen years after the victory at Dan-no-ura, he had managed to do away with all his close relatives. Yoshitsune, the hero of Dan-no-ura and the greatest warrior of all, was tracked down vindictively; and, when he finally killed his wife, his children, and himself rather than surrender, Yoritomo had his head preserved in wine and carried back to Kamakura. (One remembers Fan Li, in the fifth century B.C. in China: "When the bird is killed, one puts aside the bow . . . when the enemy is vanquished, one undoes the Minister to whom one owes the victory.")

As a result, the Minamoto clan did not remain in power for long after Yoritomo's death in 1199. The struggle over the succession resulted in his wife's family (the Hojo) becoming the real rulers of the country, ruling through members of the Minamoto family, who were still called shoguns but were no more than their puppets. The Hojo, ironically, were descended from the Taira, so that the final victory might be said to belong equally to the rival clans, even as the Wars of the Roses ended in the marriage between Lancaster and York.

In the thirteenth century Japan was faced for the first time with a threat of invasion. The Mongols had already overrun central Asia and the Middle East, striking as far as Europe; they had conquered north China, and Korea had sworn allegiance. Now they looked across the sea to Japan. Beginning in 1266, Kublai Khan sent six separate embassies to demand that the Land of the Rising Sun submit to him, as others had done. When the ruling Shogun refused, he prepared for invasion.

The Koreans were forced to build ships and provide the necessary men, equipment, and provisions, and in November 1274 a Mongol fleet of several hundred ships sailed from Korean ports. They landed first on the tiny islands of Tsushima and Iki and massacred the garrisons there, who fought to the last man. Then they sailed on to Hakata Bay, outside the Straits of Shimonoseki, and forced a landing. The Japanese put up a desperate resistance, but they were no match for the Mongol cavalry. The Mongols, moreover, were equipped with explosive weapons fired from metal tubes, which not only inflicted heavy losses but were demoralizing to men unfamiliar with explosives. The invasion might well have succeeded. The outcome, however, was decided by the weather. A sudden storm struck the coast, and the Mongols, afraid of being cut off from their ships in the gale, hastily re-embarked and retreated, with considerable losses in ships and men.

This was only the beginning. Kublai Khan sent again, and again, to demand that the Japanese submit. The Shogun ordered the Mongol envoys executed, stuck their heads on poles over the city gate, and began building up new defenses, including a stone wall round Hakata Bay.

In 1281 the Mongols mounted a second invasion, with over a hundred thousand men: Mongols, Koreans, and Chinese. They landed again at Hakata and at other points along the west coast. The new wall kept them from striking inland, but they held their beachheads on the coast for almost two months against constant attack by the Japanese. Again, more violently, the weather decided the fate of the invaders. A terrific typhoon in mid-August destroyed the greater part of the Mongol fleet. Some ships were driven ashore, others foundered at sea, and those that escaped had to sail with only the men who happened to be aboard. Those on shore were left for the Japanese to slaughter or take prisoner at their leisure.

Thus a Divine Wind, or Kamikaze, as the Japanese called it, had twice saved the country. The gods had delivered them. (Hence the name Kamikaze for the pilots who crashed their bomb-laden planes onto the decks of enemy ships during World War II, hoping to destroy these as the typhoons had destroyed the Mongols.)

The Mongols did not return again. They were preoccupied with the final conquest of China. But the Japanese continued to expect them for a dozen years and more, keeping their armed forces in a constant state of readiness. This meant a heavy economic burden, high taxes, and great hardship among the people, and it was one of the reasons for the fall of the Kamakura government early in the fourteenth century.

They were succeeded by a new shogunate, the Ashikaga, and although their strength also lay in the eastern provinces, the Ashikaga established themselves in Kyoto. Their Bakufu, or Tent Government, was set up in the Muromachi district of the capital, and the Ashikaga period is often known (especially in relation to their art) as the Muromachi. It lasted from 1336 to 1573.

These were turbulent centuries. The Ashikaga never

succeeded in gaining complete control over either the feudal chieftains or the powerful Buddhist monasteries, with their private armies. Yet it was a creative period, comparable to that of Heian, with new inspiration and freshness of feeling in both art and religion. It was then that most of the things we think of as peculiarly Japanese originated: the classical theater, the tea ceremony, flower arrangement, and landscape gardening.

These developments were largely due to Buddhist influence. It was, however, a reformed Buddhism. Over the years the rival sects of Shingon, Tendai, and the Pure Land had lost much of their meaning, and in the twelfth and thirteenth centuries there was a strong revival of faith.

A new sect, the Lotus, was founded in the thirteenth century by Nichiren, the son of a fisherman, a true reformer—fiery, intolerant, and fiercely nationalistic. Nichiren appealed strongly to the warrior class. Moreover, he predicted that if men did not accept his teachings Japan would be invaded by foreign armies, and his reputation was thus enormously enhanced by the Mongol landings.

Another new school of Buddhism had even greater influence on the military leaders. This was Zen (in Chinese, Ch'an), which was introduced to Japan during the twelfth and thirteenth centuries by monks returning from the Southern Sung court. Zen teaches meditation. Although it became the dominant sect in China and in Ashikaga Japan, it is almost closer in feeling to Taoism, with its love of nature, its simplicity, and its emphasis on individual enlightenment. Yet Zen also teaches that strict discipline, mental and physical, is necessary if one is to achieve enlightenment. And, although it might seem that a meditative sect would cause men to turn inward, losing contact with the world, quite the opposite happened. Its stress on self-reliance and character made it an ideal religion for the Japanese warrior class.

Zen philosophy combined with the innate Japanese love of beauty to create the art and culture of the Ashikaga, or Muromachi, period and, indeed, of Japan to this day. It has been described as "the cultivation of the little," the feeling that perfection lies in simplicity and form, that a single flower may be more beautiful than a garden, a few scattered rocks more significant than any building. This can, of course, be exaggerated; days of thought and effort may go into making a flower arrangement look simple. But there is no doubt of the Japanese feeling for nature or of their genius for giving beauty to simple things—a child's toy, a kitchen towel, a fan.

The tea ceremony, a complicated and leisurely ritual in which each utensil is chosen as much for beauty as for utility, was introduced during the Ashikaga period. So was the Noh Dance, or classical theater, in which every movement, every word, is so traditional that a modern performance can be as incomprehensible to most Japanese as to a foreigner. The characters of the Noh are often unreal: ghosts returning from the other world in search of revenge, or even emotions—love, jealousy, or anger—made visible. It is performed on a bare wooden platform built out into the theater, with the audience on three sides; and the actors come and go along a bridge at the left, their gorgeous costumes and stiff, formal movements in striking contrast to the simplicity of the background.

The influence of Zen was strong not only in the Noh and in the tea ceremony but in architecture, in painting, and in poetry. Artists tried to capture the whole meaning of nature in a few brush strokes, the whole of a forest in a single tree, the living world in a grasshopper or a butterfly. The best of Ashikaga, or Muromachi, painting was worthy of the Sung masters on whom the artists modeled themselves. And their genius was particularly suited to the horizontal scroll, those long paintings which are never meant to be seen all at once but are gradually unrolled, unfolding a particular story or the details of a particular scene.

Porcelain, lacquer, and damascene work (metal ornamented with gold or silver) were also of high quality. Japanese paper was extremely fine, as indeed it still is; in the seventeenth century Rembrandt preferred Japanese paper for his etchings because of its soft, warm tone.

In spite of the unsettled times the standard of living rose, agricultural production increased, and there was far more contact between different parts of the country than ever before. Trade with China and Korea flourished, although there seems to have been occasional confusion in Japanese minds between trade and piracy, and, if merchants did not make the profits they expected from the first, they might try the second.

For a short time Chinese influence was strong. In 1392 one Ashikaga shogun went so far as to become a tributary of the Chinese, acknowledging himself "subject" to the Ming Dynasty. This arrangement, however, lasted only twenty years and probably amounted to no more than a token suzerainty, useful in improving trade and diplomatic relations.

In fact, though the Japanese still had great respect for Chinese culture, Japan had now developed her own way of life, her own world, her own religion. After the fourteenth century she was increasingly independent, not only politically but culturally—an island civilization on her own. Yet, in some ways, although so insular and so cut off from the rest of the world, she remained more adaptable than her great continental neighbor. Her history showed that she could borrow from others and make what she borrowed her own. And although she resisted the influence of the West for as long as she could, when it did come she was perhaps better able to cope with it than was China.

Epilogue

At the end of the fourteenth century China, Korea, and, to some extent, Japan were entering on a period of stability which lasted into modern times. There were, of course, changes of dynasty or ruling family, intervals of chaos and confusion. There were also periods of great prosperity and great cultural and material progress. But both the upheavals and the many constructive achievements of these centuries took place within the framework of tradition. The basic social and political order was not questioned.

In China the Ming Dynasty, founded in 1368, held the Dragon Throne until 1644. Its rulers built a new capital at Peking, and the surviving temples, palaces, and gates of that ancient city date from the early fifteenth century. By the beginning of the seventeenth century the dynastic cycle had run its course; warlords fought for power, and the last Ming Emperor killed himself when the capital fell to one of these. The Manchus, a new "barbarian" tribe risen to power in the north, took advantage of this disintegration of the Ming Dynasty to conquer China and set up a dynasty of their own, the Ch'ing. They succeeded, where the Mongols had failed, in establishing their rule on a lasting basis.

In Korea the Yi Dynasty, which had consolidated the kingdom after the expulsion of the Mongols, with its capital at Seoul, was extraordinarily long-lived. Although weakened by struggles for power between rival factions, and dominated for centuries by the Manchus, it survived until 1910, when Korea was conquered by the Japanese.

In Japan the Ashikaga shoguns continued to rule the country until 1573, in theory, but their last century was one of bitter local warfare. Unity was restored by a series of strong leaders, and a new shogunate, the Tokugawa, was founded in 1603.

Meanwhile European, especially Portuguese, traders and missionaries had reached Japan during the sixteenth century, and Christianity had made many converts. In the seventeenth century, however, the Japanese rulers determined to stamp out not only Christianity but all foreign influence. Missionaries and their converts alike were persecuted, tortured, and executed. Japanese were forbidden to leave Japan, and trade with foreigners was prohibited. Japan became an island culturally as well as geographically, isolated as she had not been for over a thousand years. It was only when, in 1853, Commodore Perry, backed by a strong naval force, insisted on the Japanese agreeing to a treaty of friendship and trade with the United States that Japan reluctantly entered into relations with the West again.

Thereafter Japan adapted herself to the modern world with phenomenal speed and success. China, so much larger, and for so many centuries conscious of the overwhelming superiority of her own civilization, found it far more difficult to meet the challenge of the

West. Moreover, the impact of the Western world came at a time when the dynastic cycle was swinging low again, and the Manchu Dynasty would have been likely to collapse even without outside pressure. The Boxer Rebellion in 1900 hastened its downfall, and the regime was overthrown in 1911. A Republic of China was established, to be followed by years of civil war—an interval of chaos comparable to those which followed the downfall of the Han and the T'ang Dynasties. This was in turn succeeded by the Chinese Communists' conquest of the whole of mainland China in 1948 and 1949.

Pronunciation and Names

THE SOUNDS of the Chinese language are quite different from those of European languages—so different, in fact, that it is difficult to reproduce them at all accurately in any Western script. When one tries to "romanize" them, as the process of reproduction is called, one has to use some system—almost like a code—which will give a rough indication of how the word is pronounced. How difficult this can be is shown by the word for sun. The Chinese word is a mixture of *l*, *r*, and *j*, pronounced simultaneously, which is almost impossible to write down. The Wade system of romanization, which this book follows, writes it as *jih;* this bears very little relation to the way it is actually pronounced, but when you know some Chinese you know what it stands for.

To complicate things still further, Wade, who invented this system (other systems are even worse!), heard the *b*, *g*, *j*, and *d* sounds as like *p*, *k*, *ch*, and *t*. So he wrote them that way. When he heard what most people hear as *p*, *k*, *ch*, and *t*, he had to write them with an aspirate: *p'*, *k'*, *ch'*, and *t'*. This means that what is written as *ch'in* is pronounced approximately like our "chin" and that *chin* is roughly our "gin." *Tung* is pronounced *doong*, and *t'ung* is *tung*.

In the Wade romanization the city we know as

Peking is Pei-ching, pronounced *bey-jing*. The Chinese Nationalists call it Pei-p'ing, which is pronounced *bey-ping*. (In cases like this, however, where a geographical or personal name is well known in the West, I have not hesitated to use the most familiar form, regardless of system.)

In personal names, the Chinese, the Koreans, and, generally speaking, the Japanese put the surname first. Thus Chiang is the surname, and Kai-shek the given name. Mao Tze-tung is generally called Chairman Mao; in Western terms he could also be called Mr. Mao, or Tze-tung Mao.

Chinese emperors had all sorts of names: personal names, which they dropped when they came to the throne; reign names, which usually changed every few years; and titles given to them after their death. For example, the emperor we call Ming Huang (713–756) was born Li (his surname) Lung-chi. He became Emperor T'ang Hsuan Tsung, and Ming Huang is an abbreviation of his posthumous name.

The names of the principal Chinese dynasties are pronounced, roughly, as follows:

Ch'in = Chin
Chin = Gin
Chou = Joe
Han = Hahn (*a* as in "hard")
Sui = Sway
Sung = Soong
T'ang = Taang
Wei = Way

The Calendar

THE CHINESE CALENDAR is very ancient. The legendary Emperor Yao is said to have appointed astronomers some 4,000 years ago to study the stars, observe eclipses, and fix the exact dates of the solstices and equinoxes. (The solstices are when the sun is farthest north or south, at midwinter and midsummer; the equinoxes are when the days and nights are equal, in spring and fall.) He also ordered them to adjust the solar year and the lunar month by adding an extra month to the year whenever necessary.

This need to make an adjustment between the month, which is based on the moon, and the year, which is based on the sun, is the basic problem of all calendars. The year has 365¼ days, and the month has 29½ days, and 29½ simply will not go into 365¼. A year with twelve lunar months slips backward by approximately eleven days every year. That is why the Arab calendar, being lunar, constantly moves in relation to the seasons. The Chinese solved the difficulty by an ingenious system of slipping in extra months, called intercalary months—a sort of leap-month, used in the same way that we have an extra day in February every fourth year to take care of the fraction in the year of 365¼ days.

The spring equinox, which is, of course, a solar date, was supposed to fall in the second month of the Chinese year. When the months had slipped so far in relation to the solar year that it would have fallen in the third month, then that third month became a second second month, and the year went on from there. The same thing could happen with the summer solstice in the fifth month, the autumn equinox in the eighth, or the winter solstice in the eleventh; if they had not occurred by the time the appropriate month ended, the month was repeated. There had to be an intercalary month about every three years, and it always took the form of an additional second, fifth, eighth, or eleventh month.

Whether this was done as long ago as the reign of Yao (if Yao existed) may be questioned. During the Shang Dynasty, however (about 1523–1027 B.C.), periods of ten, twenty, or more often thirty days were already being added to keep the solar and lunar years in time. By the Han Dynasty (206 B.C.–220 A.D.) the system of inserting months at fixed intervals was already in use. With slight adjustments, it remained the official calendar until 1911, when the Chinese Republic adopted the Western (Gregorian) calendar.

Chronological Table

	CHINA	NOMADS	KOREA	JAPAN	ELSEWHERE
B.C.					
before 2000	The Model Emperors				
ca. 1994	Hsia Dynasty (? legendary)				
ca. 1523	Shang-Yin Dynasty			Ainu	The New Kingdom in Egypt
ca. 1027	Chou Dynasty				
	(Spring-Autumn Period, 722–481 B.C.			Jomon Culture	
	Warring States Period, 481–221 B.C.)				Rome founded, 753 B.C.
255	Ch'in Dynasty				Buddha, 623–543 B.C.
	Ch'in Shih Huang Ti, 247–210 B.C.				Alexander the Great, 356–323 B.C.
	(conquest of China completed, 221 B.C.)			Yayoi Culture	
206	Han Dynasty	Hsiung-nu (Huns)			
	Liu Pang (Kao Tsu), 206–195 B.C.		Chinese colonies founded, 108 B.C.		
	Wu Ti, 141–87 B.C.				Julius Caesar, 102–44 B.C.
A.D.	(usurpation of Wang Mang, 8–23 A.D.)				Jesus
23	Later Han Dynasty	Hsien-pi			
220	Three Kingdoms: Wu, Wei, Shu Han		Three Kingdoms	Tomb Culture	
			57 B.C.–668 A.D.		
265/280	Western Chin	T'o-pa		(Yamato period from about the 3rd century)	Constantine, 288–337
317	Eastern Chin (and Sixteen Kingdoms in the north)		(Koguryo, Paekche, Silla)		

	CHINA	NOMADS	KOREA	JAPAN	ELSEWHERE
86	Division between North and South: Northern Wei (386–535) Eastern Wei Western Wei Northern Ch'i Northern Chou Liu Sung Southern Ch'i Liang Ch'en	Juan-Juan			Fall of Rome, 410
89	Sui Dynasty	T'u-chüeh (Turks)		Prince Shotoku (died 621)	Mohammed, 570–632
18	T'ang Dynasty				
	T'ai Tsung, 626–649				
	Empress Wu (died 705)				
	Ming Huang 712–756		Kingdom of Silla, 668–935	Nara, 710–784	Charlemagne, 768–814
07	The Ten Kingdoms and Five Dynasties *	Khitan (Liao Dynasty)	Koryo, 935–1392	Heian-Kyo, 794–1185	
60	Sung Dynasty * (Southern Sung from 1127)	Juchen (Chin Dynasty)			Norman Conquest, 1066
		Mongols	(Mongol domination, 1259–1356)	Kamakura shoguns, 1185–1336	Crusades, 1095–1272
279	Yüan Dynasty (Mongols)	Genghiz Khan proclaimed Great Khan, 1206; died, 1227		(Yoritomo, 1185–1199)	
		Kublai Khan, Great Khan, 1260; died, 1294			
368	Ming Dynasty (to 1644)		Yi Dynasty, 1392	Ashikaga shoguns, 1336–1573	

* During the Ten Kingdoms and Five Dynasties, and during the Sung Dynasty, the greater part of north hina was ruled by two Tartar dynasties, the Khitan (called Liao by the Chinese) and the Juchen (called hin by the Chinese).

Bibliography

(Starred books are especially recommended for further reading.)

BODDE, DERK: *China's First Unifier: A Study of the Ch'in Dynasty as Seen in the Life of Li Ssu* (Leiden: E. J. Brill, 1938)

BRINKLEY, F.: *A History of the Japanese People* (New York: Encyclopaedia Britannica, 1915)

BRINKLEY, F.: *Japan: Its History, Arts and Literature* (Boston: J. P. Millet Co., 1901)

CARTER, DAGNEY: *China Magnificent* (New York: The John Day Co., 1935)

* CARTER, THOMAS F.: *The Invention of Printing in China* (New York: Columbia University Press, 1925)

COLLIS, MAURICE: *The First Holy One* (New York: Alfred A. Knopf, 1948)

CORDIER, HENRI: *Histoire Générale de la Chine* (Paris: P. Geuthner, 1920)

* CREEL, H. G.: *The Birth of China* (New York: Frederick Ungar Publishing Co., 1937)

DUBS, HOMER H.: *The History of the Former Han Dynasty, by Pan Ku* (Baltimore: Waverly Press, 1938)

DUYVENDAK, J. J. L.: *The Book of Lord Shang* (London: A. Probsthain, 1928)

* FAIRBANK, JOHN K., & REISCHAUER, EDWIN O.: *East Asia:*

The Great Tradition, vol. 1 of *A History of East Asian Civilization* (Boston: Houghton Mifflin Company, 1958)

FITZGERALD, C. P.: *China: A Short Cultural History*, revised edition (London: The Cresset Press, 1950)

GILES, H. A.: *A Chinese Biographical Dictionary* (London: Bernard Quaritch, 1898)

* GOODRICH, L. C.: *A Short History of the Chinese People* (London: George Allen & Unwin, 1957)

GROUSSET, RENÉ: *The Civilizations of the East: China* (New York: Alfred A. Knopf, 1934)

HERRMANN, A.: *An Historical Atlas of China*, revised edition (Chicago: Aldine Publishing Co., 1966)

HIRTH, F.: *The Ancient History of China* (New York: Columbia University Press, 1908)

* HUDSON, G. F.: *Europe and China* (London: Edward Arnold, 1931)

HULBERT, H. B.: *The History of Korea*, edited by C. N. Weems (London: Korea Review, 1962)

JENYNS, SOAME (translator): *Selections from the Three Hundred Poems of the T'ang Dynasty* (London: John Murray, 1940)

KENNEDY, MALCOLM: *A Short History of Japan* (New York: Mentor Books, 1963)

LANCHESTER, GEORGE: *The Yellow Emperor's South-Pointing Chariot* (Lecture to the China Society, London, February 3, 1947)

LATOURETTE, KENNETH: *The Chinese, Their History and Culture* (New York: The Macmillan Co., 1934)

LATTIMORE, OWEN: *Inner Asian Frontiers of China* (New York: Oxford University Press, 1940)

LEGGE, JAMES: *The Sacred Books of China*, five volumes (Oxford: Oxford University Press, 1879)

LIU WU-CHI: *A Short History of Confucian Philosophy* (London: Pelican Books, 1955)

LUM, PETER: *The Purple Barrier: The Story of the Great Wall of China* (London: Robert Hale, 1960)

MAILLA, PÈRE J. DE: *Histoire Générale de la Chine* (Paris: P. D. Pierres, 1779)

MARCO POLO: see Polo, Marco

MARTIN, H. D.: *The Rise of Chingis Khan, and His Conquest of North China* (Baltimore: The Johns Hopkins Press, 1950)

MAYERS, WILLIAM F.: *Chinese Reader's Manual* (Shanghai: Presbyterian Mission Press, 1924)

° MCCUNE, EVELYN: *The Arts of Korea* (Tokyo: Charles E. Tuttle Co., 1962)

MCCUNE, GEORGE: *Korea Today* (Cambridge: Harvard University Press, 1950)

° MORRIS, IVAN: *The World of the Shining Prince* (London: Oxford University Press, 1964)

MURASAKI, LADY: *The Tale of Genji,* translated by Arthur Waley (Boston: Houghton Mifflin Co., 1925)

NEEDHAM, JOSEPH: *Science and Civilization in China* (Cambridge: Cambridge University Press; seven volumes, not yet completed; first volume, 1954)

NELSON, M. F.: *Korea and the Old Orders in Eastern Asia* (Baton Rouge: Louisiana State University Press, 1946)

PAYNE, ROBERT (editor): *The White Pony: An Anthology of Chinese Poetry* (New York: The John Day Co., 1947)

POLO, MARCO: *Description of the World,* translated as *The Travels of Marco Polo* by R. E. Latham (London: Penguin Books, 1958)

REISCHAUER, EDWIN O.: see Fairbank, John K.

SAEKI, P. Y.: *The Nestorian Monument in China* (New York: The Macmillan Co., 1916)

° SANSOM, SIR GEORGE: *A History of Japan to 1334* (Stanford: Stanford University Press, 1958)

SANSOM, SIR GEORGE: *Japan—A Short Cultural History* (London: The Cresset Press, 1931)

SEI SHONAGON: *The Pillow Book of Sei Shonagon,* translated by Arthur Waley (Boston: Houghton Mifflin Co., 1929)

SSU-MA CH'IEN: *Statesman, Patriot and General in Ancient China,* translated by Derk Bodde (New Haven: American Oriental Society, 1940)

STEIN, SIR MARC AUREL: *On Ancient Central Asian Tracks* (London: Macmillan & Co., 1933)

* STORRY, RICHARD: *Japan* (Oxford: Oxford University Press, 1965; in Modern World Series)

TSAO, HSUEH-CHIN: *Dream of the Red Chamber,* translated by Chi-Chen Wang (New York: Doubleday & Co., 1958)

WALEY, ARTHUR: *Life and Times of Po Chu-I* (London: George Allen & Unwin, 1949)

WALEY, ARTHUR (translator): *One Hundred and Seventy Chinese Poems* (London: Constable & Co., 1918)

WALEY, ARTHUR: *The Poetry and Career of Li Po* (London: George Allen & Unwin, 1950)

WIEGER, LEO: *A History of the Religious Beliefs and Philosophical Opinions in China,* translated by E. C. Werner (China: Hsien-Hsien Press, 1927)

WIEGER, LEO: *Textes Historiques* (China: Hien-Hien, 1903)

WILLETTS, WILLIAM: *Chinese Art,* two volumes (London: Penguin Books, 1958)

WITTFOGEL, KARL A.: *Oriental Despotism* (New Haven: Yale University Press, 1957)

WU CH'ENG-EN: *Monkey,* translated by Arthur Waley (London: George Allen & Unwin, 1942)

Index